GOD'S WISDOM
REVEALED

GOD'S WISDOM REVEALED

KENNY ROBERTS

TATE PUBLISHING
AND ENTERPRISES, LLC

Published by Tate Publishing & Enterprises, LLC
127 E. Trade Center Terrace | Mustang, Oklahoma 73064 USA
1.888.361.9473 | www.tatepublishing.com

Tate Publishing is committed to excellence in the publishing industry. The company reflects the philosophy established by the founders, based on Psalm 68:11,
"The Lord gave the word and great was the company of those who published it."

Book design copyright © 2014 by Tate Publishing, LLC. All rights reserved.
Cover design by Gian Philipp Rufin
Interior design by Jomel Pepito

Published in the United States of America

ISBN: 978-1-63185-536-8
1. Religion / Biblical Studies / Old Testament
2. Religion / Biblical Studies / General
14.05.16

Contents

PREFACE

A few years ago, I set into motion a chain of events that led me to begin an in-depth study of the Bible. I, like the biblical Job, had gotten way too full of myself and became a little arrogant, even with our Lord. I remember that day well. At work, a major project was nearing completion, and I was on my way to make some final checks and adjustments to a robotics parts-loader that I had designed and was having fabricated at a machine shop in Tulsa, Oklahoma. Everything was coming together nicely, and I was about to complete the largest project of my career. However, I could not stay focused on the business at hand because my mind kept drifting to thoughts of what I should be doing for the Lord. I became so annoyed at the distraction that I began complaining about it. I raved at God and said something like this: "I'm awfully busy here, give me some slack. If there's something that you want me to do, show me what it is, and I'll do it. Give me the desire to do it and then *make it happen*!" You know, you should think about what you're going to say, *before* you start talking to our Lord. This book is a result of that answered prayer.

God's Wisdom Revealed contains the Old Testament Book of Job, abridged and revised, from the 1611 edition of the King James Version of the Holy Bible. It includes a definition of rarely used words and phrases and a brief description of how people lived around twenty-five hundred years ago. It also includes comments from time to time in an effort to make the story of Job easier to follow.

Do a little research and you will discover that sometime between the first edition of the King James Version of the Holy Bible and the Americanized versions of the King James Bible, some mistakes were made in spelling and punctuation. These errors, likely made by the typesetters that worked for the printers, have made the Book of Job an impossible story to learn and understand, unless you correct the mistakes. That is why this account of the Old Testament Book of Job is according to the 1611 edition of the King James Version of the Holy Bible as it was published by Thomas Nelson Publishers, Nashville, Tennessee in 1989.

Two of these mistakes changed the meaning of two passages and put an entirely different slant on the Old Testament Book of Job. Contrary to popular belief; Job was not a patient man, there is no reference to a battle with Satan over Job, and the Book of Job is not a story about why bad things happen to good people just to test or strengthen their faith. So get ready for a brand new story about an exceptionally good man who learned some very tough lessons the hard way.

These mistakes were discovered while I was changing the version of the King James Bible that I was studying so that it would match the original 1611 edition. That was because I wanted to avoid infringing on someone's copyright should I ever finish this book. And I have always found that the closer you get to the original story, the more accurate that version will be. Included herein is all the information that you will need to verify the accuracy of my work.

One of these mistakes is at Job chapter 24, verse 1, which is worded like this in the original King James Bible: "Why, seeing Times are not hidden from the Almighty, doe they, that know him not, see his dayes?" (Job 24:1, KJV 1611). In other words: Why do some people who do *not* know God have health, wealth, and happiness? In some of the latter editions of the King James Bible, two commas have been removed. Now, the same passage reads: "Why, seeing times are not hidden from the Almighty, do they that know him not see his days?" (Job 24:1, KJV present-day). In other words: Why do some people that *know God* fail to have health, wealth, and happiness? There is a vast difference between knowing God and not knowing Him! This is a very important passage because it is used to support the belief that bad things happen to good people to test their faith. Bad things may happen to test our faith, but this passage does not support that point of view. In the original passage, Job is complaining because he thinks that God should be punishing the ungodly that have health, wealth, and happiness instead of him. Check the Scriptures that follow and you will discover that they refer to persons that do not know God.

Then at Job 41:8, the word *battell* was replaced with the word *battle*, while *battle* is the correct pronunciation of the word, which is spelled as b-a-t-t-e-l-l, it is not the correct meaning in this passage. The word *battell*, now spelled b-a-t-t-e-l, actually refers to a list of debts owed. The University of Oxford in England, where the King James Bible originated, may still call their students' charge account a *battell*, as in: I didn't have any money when I went to eat, so I told the clerk to put it on my *battell*. And in the two places where the word, which does mean *battle*, is used to describe a fight of some kind, it is spelled as b-a-t-t-a-i-l-e. In the passage, "Lay thine hand vpon him, remember the battell: doe no more" (Job 41:8 KJV 1611). God is the one speaking and He is telling us to keep Satan at bay and to remember that He is keeping track of Satan's debts and for us to do no more than this. Check the Scriptures that follow the passage at Job 41:8, and you will discover that God goes on to tell us that one day, He is going to repay Satan for all of his misdeeds. For God said: "Who hath prevented me, that I should repay him? Whatsoever is under the whole heaven is mine" (Job 41:11, KJV present-day).

One of the things that will lead to a misunderstanding of a given Scripture is to go to the wrong source to define the meaning of words. The King James Version of the Holy Bible originated in Oxford, England over four hundred years ago and was first printed in 1611. So the only dependable source to determine what the King James Linguists meant by the use of a word is the Oxford English Dictionary. And because some words have a dual meaning, one must do a little research within the same book to determine which definition should be used. It was easy to determine the meaning of *battell* in Job because the word *battaile* was used to mean *battle*, thus leaving only one definition for the word *battell*. This was necessary because *battell* is used to mean battle in some of the other books of the Bible.

The following passages from the 1611 edition of the KJV are where the words *battell* and the word *battaile* spelled b a t t a i l e are located in the Old Testament Book of Job. Now, the correct pronunciation of both these words is the same with *battle*, but I pronounce the word spelled b a t t e l l as ba'tell to distinguish the two words.

In Job 15:24, it reads: "Trouble and anguish shall make him afraid; they shall preuaile against him, as a king ready to the battell." The king checks to see who is indebted to him, which would be a natural preparation in times of trouble.

In Job 38:23, it reads: "Which I haue reserued against the time of trouble, against the day of battaile and warre?" This is self-explanatory.

In Job 39:25, it reads: "Hee saith among the trumpets, Ha, ha: and he smelleth the battaile afarre off, the thunder of the captaines, and the shouting." Again, this is self-explanatory.

And in Job 41:8, it reads: "Lay thine hand vpon him, remember the battell: doe no more." Now, God is speaking here, so *him* in this passage is referring to Satan, and the *battell* is the record of his debts.

Should you wish to check this out for yourself, you will only need two things: A reprinting of the 1611 edition of the King James Version of the Holy Bible, which is available either from Hendrickson Publishers, Inc. *or* Thomas Nelson Publishers, or a facsimile reproduction of an original 1611 edition of The King James Version of the Holy Bible can be obtained from greatsite.com, which is the online showroom of The Bible Museum in Arizona. And you will also need either a very old Webster's Unabridged Dictionary that was published before 1969, or a very old Unabridged American English Dictionary, or the Oxford English Dictionary that is mainly used in England. However, the word meaning battle that is spelled b a t t a i l e will only be found in the Oxford English Dictionary. And if you have a good dictionary app in your smartphone, you will find the word spelled b a t t e l there.

Check the history of the King James Bible and you will find that James Charles Stuart became the King of England in 1603 when his mother Queen Elizabeth died, and that he remained the king until his death on March 27, 1625. King James knew that only a very few people could still read and understand the old Bible manuscripts. So in 1604, to ensure that an accurate version of the Bible stories would be preserved in English, he appointed a group of around fifty-five men to translate the ancient words and compare their work to the work of others, and then assemble the stories into one book. The men he appointed to this task were not only the best linguists and scholars in the kingdom but also in the world. King James was also an accomplished linguist, and the men that he appointed to translate the Bible manuscripts to English almost certainly knew that he had studied the ancient writings. I suspect the translators were very careful to preserve the original meaning of the Scriptures, knowing that the king would likely check their work. I just wish that the people that have rewritten, and those who will rewrite the bible, had the same incentive to get it right.

INTRODUCTION

The Old Testament Book of Job is a story about a very prosperous man named Job, who lived around twenty-five hundred years ago. Job had about everything a man could want. He was very wealthy, he had a nice large family, lots of political clout, self-confidence, self-esteem, and he feared and worshiped God. By the common measure of a man today, Job would be judged perfect and upright, very wealthy in all respects. And, Job really was a very good man, and he did keep all the ordinances of God, and he was well-respected by all walks of life. However, he had a flaw in his personality that was not pleasing to God. This is a story about how God corrected that flaw and taught Job how to be the kind of man that he thought he was.

This book corrects mistakes made in the Old Testament Book of Job during the many reprints of the original King James Version of The Holy Bible. It also prepares the reader for a study of the New Testament by showing how God interacted with man before Jesus became our Lord and changed a few of the laws of God.

The publisher has asked that I add which translation I used for each Scripture cited in this book, and since I am the only one that revised and abridged the wording of the Scripture in the Book of Job, which is from the original King James Version of the Holy Bible, I am not sure what to do. All I can say is that this version of the Old Testament Book of Job is not intended to be a new version of the Book of Job, but a tool for learning and understanding the King James Version of the Old Testament Book of Job. For purposes of this book, when the text is from the part of the Old Testament Book of Job that I revised, it will be identified as to where it came from and labeled "KRV", which will stand for Kenny Roberts Version. When the text is marked "KJV present-day", it will be text from the King James Version commonly used today. And when the text is marked "KJV 1611" it will be from the 1611 edition of the King James Version of the Holy Bible as it was published by Thomas Nelson Publishers, Nashville in 1989. And the wording of the passages has been verified to agree with a facsimile reproduction of an original 1611 King James Version of the Holy Bible as published by The Bible Museum in Litchfield Park, Arizona.

This paragraph is included should the author read the audio version of this book: The bible teaches us that we have all received certain gifts from God. I believe that a strong desire to learn things well enough to understand is a gift from God. But I'm going to tell you right up front that reading or performing a book on tape is not one of mine. However, the Old Testament Book of Job will be much easier to follow and understand if it is read to you by someone who is familiar with the somewhat confusing way that it is worded and punctuated. So suffer me a little, and I will do the best that I can.

THE DAYS OF JOB

The story of Job is about many things. It is about the meaning and value of wisdom and understanding. It is about our tendency to hunt for reasons why whenever bad things happen, and how we usually jump to the wrong conclusions. It is about being quick to look for the bad in a person, but slow to consider the good. It is also about the power that Satan has over us if we fail to please God. But the Old Testament Book of Job is mainly about a very common personality trait called *pride*, that can get you into a lot of trouble with our Lord.

Furthermore, the story answers questions that some people ask when they suffer or see someone else suffer. Questions like, why is God letting this happen? Or, why is God doing these things? Many inquiries about God that begin with *why* are answered in this story. Moreover, it teaches us a great deal about the early relationship between God and man. Knowing how God interacted with man before Jesus died on the cross will make many of the passages in the New Testament easier to understand. One of the more remarkable things about the Book of Job is that it gives us a glimpse of the relationship between God and Satan. And, like the first four books of the New Testament that contain the words of Jesus, the book of Job contains the words of God.

The Book of Job is also one of those stories where the ending clears up what happens in the beginning. Therefore, I will be making comments from time to time in an effort to make the story easier to follow. You also have a tendency to get lost in the confusing wording; therefore, I have shortened some of the long drawn-out speeches and rephrased some of the passages to make the Old Testament story of Job easier to follow. I have also changed a few of the words to the more commonly used ones that convey the same meaning. However, there are a few words and phrases that I have not changed because doing so might alter the meaning of the Scripture or make it more confusing than it already is. Let's go over some of these words and phrases and consider what their meaning was around twenty-five hundred years ago.

Or to be more exact, let us consider what these words meant to the linguists and scholars that translated the old Bible Manuscripts to English a little over four hundred years ago.

Iniquity is a word that is used very often in the Book of Job. If you pass by someone that needs help without rendering it, you will be committing an *iniquity*. You would have to put many words together to have the same meaning as *iniquity*. Words like unjust, evil, criminal, sinful, immoral, cruelty, corruption, bad, and wickedness are just a few of the synonyms for *iniquity*. So if you have committed *iniquity*, watch out.

If you were to *rent your mantle*, then you would tear your outer garment with your bare hands to demonstrate your disgust at what was said or at what has happened. The practice of renting one's mantle to show disgust is still a common practice in some parts of the world. There are even those that will sew the seams of their clothes with very weak thread so the material will not be ruined when they rip it apart at the seams. And imagine the humiliation if you tried to *rent your mantle* and were not strong enough to tear it.

Your *tabernacle* is a place held sacred and it is usually considered a temporary shelter. Our soul is said to *tabernacle* in the body because it only dwells there while we are alive. A tent that you live in could also be called your tabernacle. The portable sanctuary carried by the Jews in their wanderings from Egypt to Palestine and later the Jewish temple was called a *tabernacle*.

If you were to *abase* someone, then you would be degrading him. *Abase* also means to disgrace, dishonor, and humiliate. Please, do not abase me for trying to make the story of Job easier to learn and understand.

If you were to *abhor* yourself, then you would not have a very high opinion of your character. You might *abhor* something that you said in anger. I *abhor* some of the things that I did in the past, and now I'm trying to make up for them.

If you were to *assuage* someone, you might be trying to lessen his grief. *Assuage* also means to alleviate, soothe, ease, and mitigate. Let me *assuage* your mind and assure you that I have retained the original meaning of the Book of Job in the abridgement and revision of this story.

If you were to *eschew* evil, you would be keeping away from it, even though temptations to sin are all around you. *Eschew* also means to abstain from, avoid, shun, or refrain from doing something. The desire for riches of this world is something that is very difficult to *eschew*.

If you are a *vile* person, then you need to change your ways, for if you were *vile*, you would be wicked, contemptible, cheap, sinful, and offensive. A *vile* person will not hesitate to take advantage of someone nice.

The word *sanctified* can mean many different things. In this story, I believe the word means to give sanction to or approval of something, and to cause someone to be respected, loved, and revered, which is the meaning of the word *sanctify*. If your father sent and *sanctified* you, then you would know that he approves of what you are doing and that he loves you very much.

Reproach is to bring shame and disgrace upon someone, and it can also mean to accuse someone of a wrong. *Reproach* also means to discredit, revile, condemn, disapprove, criticize, and dishonor. I *reproach* myself for putting off an in-depth study of the Bible.

Supplication means to make a request or an appeal to someone, or to make a prayer to God. Should you already have an opinion formed about the messages contained in the Book of Job, I make my *supplication* to you and ask that you read and/or listen to this with an open mind.

The word *battell* is only used twice in the Book of Job, but it has caused much misunderstanding because it has been replaced with the word *battle*. The correct pronunciation of the word *battell* is actually the same with *battle*, but it is not referring to a fight of any kind. *Battell*, as used in the old English fashion, actually refers to a charge account at the University of Oxford in England, where the King James Bible originated. (I didn't have any money when I went to eat, so I told the clerk to put it on my *battell*.) The Old Testament story of Job does refer to a battle of some kind in two different passages, but the word there is spelled as b-a-t-t-a-i-l-e.

If you were to *put forth your hand*, you would be removing it from something (*Put forth your hands* from the steering wheel of your car when you're doing sixty and you might have a wreck). I pray that Jesus will never *put forth His hands* from us.

If you were to *lay your hands* on someone, you would be trying to keep them at bay or from doing evil to you. If you do not want someone to do evil to another, you might *lay your hands* on that person. If you have enough authority over someone then all you would have to do is tell that person: Do not *lay your hands* on him or her. You may want to *lay your hands* on someone that wronged you, but please leave that up to Jesus and His Father.

To *throw dust in the air* was a sign of mourning, and to *sit in dust and ashes* was a sign of extreme misfortune.

You would also have to *sit in dust and ashes* to repent for your bad behavior.

If someone were to tell you to *hold your peace*, they would want you to relax and keep your mouth shut. You would also know that the person who told you to *hold your peace* only has goodwill toward you. So *hold your peace*, and I will help you learn and understand the Old Testament Book of Job.

The Sons of God is a phrase that is used three times in the Old Testament Book of Job. And if you have read one of the latest revisions of the New Testament, you may wonder just what these words mean. That is because some of them say that Jesus is the one and only Son of God. Jesus is the only Son of God that was begotten of man, but He is certainly not God's one and only Son. You would have to disregard a whole bunch of Scriptures to believe that Jesus is the one and only Son of God.

The word *Loe* used at the beginning of a sentence means that something very important is about to be said (*Loe*, there are at least three things that you should know very well: a useful skill; the basic laws of the land that you live in; and the teachings of Jesus and His Father). The story of Job will help you learn about the Father and His teachings.

Also, the story of Job will be much easier to learn and understand if you will consider how people lived way back then. We know that the Book of Job was written about a man that lived before Jesus because it is an Old Testament story, and they were still making *burnt offerings* to God. Making *burnt offerings* was very common, and even required, in Job's day.

Everyday life was much different 2,500 years ago. Job probably lived in the most modern part of the world at that time. Some of the more affluent and highly educated could even read and write. They didn't have pen and paper as we do today. The words would have been tooled in leather or scribed in clay or scratched on the bark of certain reeds and trees or chiseled in stone by an instrument they called an *iron pen*. The engravings would have been leaded in if the words were to be preserved. The person that documented the words and stories was called a scribe. A single page would have taken a long time to inscribe and it may have been well over an eighth-of-an-inch thick. Back then, it would have taken about a week to copy even a very short book. It would have been rather heavy and very costly considering that it took a highly educated person to make copies. Books were very scarce, and only a few could afford them.

They didn't have a post office like we do today, but more than likely a fast runner or a rider called a *Post* delivered verbal and written messages very swiftly. The *Post* likely had a place to go to in each city, and when someone was seen at the designated spot, maybe a post in the ground, they would know that a message had arrived. News would have traveled very slowly and usually by word of mouth.

The only clothing would have been made from animal skins or handmade cloth. The thread or twine used to make the cloth was likely made from handspun sheep wool or other animal hair. The cloth was made by moving the woof thread through the warp thread with a *shuttle* to make the web. The *shuttle* was twine wound on a bobbin and was called the woof thread. The warp thread was strung in a manner that would allow every other thread to be separated in either direction, thus warping the thread as the cloth was made. The weaver would toss the *shuttle* from hand to hand through the V formed by separating the threads, and a good weaver would become very fast with this toss.

The flour for bread was ground in a mill consisting of two very hard stones—one on top of the other. The bottom stone was called the *nether millstone* and was the harder of the two stones. The whole grain was placed on the *nether millstone*, and when the top stone was rotated, the grain was ground into flour from the slip between the two stones.

The roads back then were nothing more than well-traveled routes and were called *ways*. You might have said, "You can get there on this *way*." If you were to describe a wilderness area, you might say that it had no *way*. The word *way* is also used in the same way that it is commonly used today.

The most common mode of transportation, other than the feet, was probably on an ass or camel's back or in a cart pulled by oxen. A trip of fifty miles in one day was a very strenuous undertaking twenty-five hundred years ago. I doubt if many ventured more than a few miles from where they were born during their entire lifetime.

People are about the only thing that hasn't changed, for we are very much the same now as we were then. We still have the same personality problems and we interact with each other in much the same manner. When we get together to discuss important topics, the one speaking usually stands up. When something solemn is spoken or you wish to emphasize your words, it is common to see someone clasp their hands together and only one person will speak at a time. This is how I picture the main settings in the Book of Job.

Job's Torments

The story of Job is told like many stories are today. It starts out by telling us a little about the star of the story and then it establishes his character by putting him through terrible tribulations and verbal abuse. Job learns a very tough lesson, changes his attitude, and then wins out in the end. In this story, three of Job's friends have a discussion with him about his great sufferings, and then a young man with wisdom from God steps in and clearly shows Job and these three men the error of their ways. After this, God shows up and teaches Job and his three friends some very important lessons.

At the beginning of the story, we find God talking to Satan about how good a man Job is, and it appears that He is bragging, but common sense should tell you that God is way above bragging. There was a very different reason for God's comments to Satan, for you see, Job had a flaw in his personality that was not pleasing to God. This particular flaw is the worst kind a person can have because the flaw itself usually keeps us from seeing it. And it was so deeply embedded in Job's personality that drastic measures were needed to correct it. Modern psychology teaches us that the only way you can change a person's behavior is by creating a significant emotional event in their life. In this story, God deceives Satan and tricks him into creating an emotional event in Job's life that will be significant enough to make Job want to change his ways.

Satan is actually deceived by God and tricked into helping Him teach Job a very tough lesson. The devil is easy to fool because he really isn't very bright; maybe that's why they call him the Prince of Darkness! If Satan were smarter, I don't believe he would have been as willing to help God. That is, because Job goes on to be the kind of man that Satan hates so much. Just keep in mind that God's wisdom is extremely great and without bounds and that He does not do wicked things to mankind; however, that does not mean that God will protect us from Satan if we fail to please Him. Get bad enough, and God may point the devil in the direction of your doorstep like he does to Job.

Much research, study, and prayer for understanding is required to learn and understand the bible. Looking up the meaning of the words used in a passage is usually enough to clarify the meaning, but when that doesn't work, one must pray for understanding. The answer to my inquiries has come in various ways. I remember one time when I was having trouble understanding the meaning of "Sufficient unto the day is the evil thereof," which is the last sentence in the passage at Matthew 6:34 (KJV present-day). That night I prayed for understanding. The next day, while driving to Dallas in a heavily loaded big truck, I came to an area where the right lane was closed. Everyone was lined up in the left lane when I noticed someone way back behind me pull out of line and head for that safety gap that I was leaving between me and the car in front. By the time he got there, I had closed that gap and kept it closed so he couldn't get back in line. He looked at me, and I shook my head at him. Then that verse rang loudly in my hearing, and I understood the meaning: "There is enough evil in the world already, don't add to it!"

I have prayed for the understanding of many Scriptures and have made every effort to retain the original meaning in the 1611 edition of the KJV; nevertheless, you are encouraged to compare this version of the story of Job with the present-day King James Version of the Holy Bible (KJV).

Now to the Old Testament Book of Job, abridged and revised from the original King James Version of the Holy Bible. We'll begin at Job 1:1.

> There was a man who lived in the land of Uz, whose name was Job. He was perfect and upright and he feared God and eschewed evil. And there were born unto him seven sons, and three daughters. Job was a man of great substance, he had seven thousand sheep, three thousand camels, five hundred yoke of oxen, and five hundred she asses, and a very great household; so much, so that this man was the greatest of all the men of the East. And his sons had great feasts in their houses and would send for their three sisters to eat and to drink with them. And during the days of their feasting Job sent and sanctified them. He also rose up early each morning and offered burnt offerings to the Lord, according to the number of them all. For Job said, It may be that my sons have sinned, and cursed God in their hearts. Thus did Job continually.

> Job 1:1–5 (KRV)

Now, I picture Job and his wife as being middle-aged and of medium build, maybe a little on the stocky side. Job has a salt-and-pepper beard, his hair is graying around the edges, and there are streaks of gray in his wife's hair. His children are above average in appearance, ranging in age from around fifteen to twenty-five. Okay, back to the Scriptures at Job 1:6.

Now, there was a day when the sons of God came to present themselves before the Lord, and Satan came also among them. And the Lord said unto Satan, from whence commest thou? Then Satan answered the Lord, and said, from going to and fro in the earth, and from walking up and down in it. And the Lord said unto Satan, have you considered my servant Job, that there is none like him in the earth, a perfect and an upright man, one that fears God and eschews evil? Then Satan answered the Lord and said, Does Job fear God for naught? Have you not made a hedge about him, and about his house, and about all that he has on every side to protect him? You have blessed the work of his hands, and his wealth has increased in the land. But put forth your hand now, and touch all that he has, and he will curse you to your face. And the Lord said unto Satan, Behold, all that he has is in your power, only do not lay your hand upon him. So Satan went forth from the presence of the Lord.

And there came a day when Job's sons and his daughters were eating and drinking wine in their eldest brother's house: And a messenger came to Job, and said, the oxen were plowing, and the asses feeding beside them, and the Sabeans attacked them, and took the oxen and asses away. Furthermore, they slayed the servants with the edge of the sword. I am the only one that escaped, and I alone have come to tell you. While he was yet speaking, there came also another, and said, The fire of God is fallen from heaven, and has burned up the sheep, and the servants, and consumed them. I am the only one that escaped, and I alone have come to tell you. While he was yet speaking, there came also another, and said, three bands of the Chaldeans came and fell upon the camels and have carried them away. Furthermore, they slayed the servants with the edge of the sword. I am the only one that escaped, and I alone have come to tell you. While he was yet speaking, there came also another, and said, your sons and your daughters were eating and drinking wine in their eldest brother's house: And, behold, there came a great wind from the wilderness, and smote the four corners of the house, and it fell upon the young men, and they are dead. I am the only one that escaped, and I alone have come to tell you.

Then Job arose, and rent his mantle, and shaved his head, and fell down upon the ground, and worshipped, and said, Naked came I out of my mother's womb and naked shall I return to the earth: the Lord gave, and the Lord has taken away, blessed be the name of the Lord. In all this, Job did not sin, nor did he charge God, or blame Him foolishly.

Job 1:6–22 (KRV)

There is a lot to be learned from this Old Testament story. For instance: Some say that Jesus is the "one and only Son of God." While Jesus is the only Son of God who was born of a woman, He is certainly not the one and only Son of God. If you choose to believe that Jesus is the one and only Son of God, then how do you account for the passage at Job 1:6 and the passage at Job 2:1? Also, to help you understand this story, don't confuse the Lord of Job with Jesus. To put it in perspective, just remember that Jesus has been Lord over the earth ever since He died on the Cross, and that God is, and always has been, Lord over the universe. I think this Scripture says it best: "For there is one

God, and one mediator between God and men, the man Christ Jesus;" (1 Timothy 2:5 KJV present-day).

Back to the story of Job (Job 2:1).

> Again there was a day when the sons of God came to present themselves before the Lord, and Satan came also among them to present himself before the Lord. And the Lord said unto Satan, from whence commest thou? And Satan answered the Lord, and said, from going to and fro in the earth, and from walking up and down in it. And the Lord said unto Satan, have you considered my servant Job, that there is none like him in the earth; a perfect and an upright man, one that fears God and eschews evil? And still he holds fast to his integrity, even though you moved me against him, to let you destroy him without cause. And Satan answered the Lord, and said, skin for skin, yea all that a man has, he will give for his life. But put forth your hand now, and touch his bone and his flesh, and he will curse you to your face. And the Lord said unto Satan, Behold, he is in your hand, but save his life.
>
> So Satan went forth from the presence of the Lord, and smote Job with sore boils, from the sole of his foot unto his crown. And Job took a potsherd to scrape himself with; and he sat down

among the ashes. Then his wife said unto him, do you still retain your integrity? Curse God, and die. But he said unto her, you are speaking like a foolish woman, what? Shall we receive good at the hand of God, and shall we not receive evil also? In all this Job did not sin with his lips.

Now, when Job's three friends heard of all this evil that was come upon him, they came, every one from his own place. Eliphaz the Temanite, and Bildad the Shuhite, and Zophar the Naamathite: for they had made an appointment together to come to mourn with him, and to comfort him. And when they lifted up their eyes and saw him from afar off, and knew him not, they raised their voice in anguish and wept; and every one of them rent his mantle, and sprinkled dust upon his head toward heaven.

Job 2:1–12 (KRV)

In other words, they knew it was Job, but they did not recognize him because of his infirmities. Then they threw dust in the air to show that they mourned for him. "So they sat down with Job upon the ground seven days and seven nights, and none spake a word unto him: for they saw that his grief was very great" (Job 2:13, KJV present-day).

Job must have been quite a sight, sitting there scraping his crusty sores with a piece of broken pottery. And he must have been a very stubborn man and well-set in his ways, for even after all this, he still believes that he is perfect and upright. He reminds me of the man who had a stubborn mule: After he got the mule harnessed and ready for work, he'd grab a club and hit him between the eyes. When asked why he did that, he answered, "He's a very good mule and a strong worker and he'll do about anything I ask, but first of all, you've got to get his attention." It is unfortunate, but many of us have to suffer before we learn to pay attention to the things of God. At times, it is really difficult to see the wisdom in God's actions, but if you will search for it, you will find it, because wisdom is always there to be found.

Job's Lamentation

God has just described Job as a man that has integrity, and integrity is a word that is also used very often in the Book of Job. If you were a man of integrity, then you would have a whole bunch of wonderful traits in your personality. You would always be compassionate toward others no matter who they were or what their lot in life is. You would be the type of person who would stop and help anyone you saw that looked like they might need a little help. Although, it is common to see people who think they have integrity pass by someone on the street with a hand out. Ask them why they do that, and they will likely tell you that if you give them money, they will just buy cigarettes or booze with it. Jesus let us know how people of integrity should act in the story about the Good Samaritan and when He told us: "Judge not, and ye shall not be judged:

condemn not, and ye shall not be condemned: forgive, and ye shall be forgiven:" (Luke 6:37, KJV present-day). In the Bible, integrity is a word that carries a lot of weight with it because honor, righteousness, honesty, incorruption, purity, and virtue are just a few of the words needed to describe integrity. So think about your integrity when you see a panhandler and just remember; how you treat that person may be how Jesus will treat you someday.

There is a little story about ministers of God's Word that I would like to pass along. This happened to me while I was serving in the navy and stationed at the Sangley Point Naval Base that used to be located next to the city of Cavite in the Philippines. A friend had rented a car, complete with driver, and asked me if I would like to tour Manila with him. We really didn't know where to go, so we asked our driver to take us to places of interest. One of the places that he took us to was likely the largest church in Manila.

Our driver knew one of the men at the church and he took us on a guided tour. While we were up in the bell tower, our tour guide told us a story about all the ministers that had been invited there. I think he mentioned Billy Graham and Oral Roberts but didn't hold me to that. Anyway, he said that they would always have someone, which was likely one of their preacher's sons, dress up in raggedy garb, and then put dirt all over him and have him pretend to be a lowly vagrant lying beside the road that led back to the airport. He said they figured that if the minister was who he held himself to be, then he would do what the Good Samaritan did and stop and help this person. He also said that if that ever happened, then that minister would have been invited back. He also said that none had ever been invited back.

Now, I see Job's three friends as being well-dressed men, very old and gray-headed, with white beards, and wrinkled skin. They are sitting on sheepskins or other animal pelts in a semicircle facing Job. Job is sitting on a pile of dirt and ashes with his legs crossed and opposite his friends. He is dressed in yellowing sackcloth that looks like old gunnysacks draped over a very gruesome-looking man. His head and body are covered with crusty sores, and he is a pitiful sight. There is also a young man named Elihu in their company. I picture them as sitting in the shade of a large overhanging rock, near the river Jordan. This is the first round of talks between Job and his three friends. We now go to Job's opening statement.

After this, Job arose and opened his mouth in anger and cursed the day he was born. And Job spake, and said, Let the day perish, wherein I was born, and the night in which it was said, there is a man-child conceived. Let that day be darkness; let not God regard it from above, neither let the light shine upon it.

Job 3:1–4 (KRV)

Why is light given to him that is in misery, and life unto the bitter in soul; which long for death, but it does not come; and they dig for it more than for hidden treasures. Do they not greatly rejoice, and are glad, when they can find the grave? Why is the light of life given to a man, whose way is hid, and whom God has hedged in? For my heaving sighs comes before I eat, and my raspy breaths are poured out like the roaring waters. For the thing, which I greatly feared, is come upon me, and that, which I was afraid of, is come unto me. I was not in safety, neither had I rest, neither was I quiet: yet trouble came.

Job 3:20–26 (KRV)

Job must have looked much worse than his friends had imagined, for their attitude has changed from that of "Let us comfort him" to "Anyone that looks this bad must have done something wrong, so let's condemn him instead." You also need to know what God said about Job's friends at the end of this story to fully understand their conversation. For the Lord said to Eliphaz the Temanite: "My wrath is kindled against thee, and against thy two friends: for ye have not spoken of me the thing that is right, as my servant Job hath" (Job 42:7, KJV present-day). So keep in mind that God did not think very highly of Job's old friends.

Now, let us return to the story where Job is just sitting back down. Each of his three old friends, Eliphaz, Bildad, and Zophar, will now begin to take turns trying to convince Job that God is punishing him because he is evil and wicked. Eliphaz speaks first, so he is likely the oldest (Job 4:1).

> Then Eliphaz the Temanite answered and said, If we commune with thee to examine your troubles, you may be grieved, but who can withhold himself from speaking? Behold, you have instructed many, and you have strengthened the weak hands. Thy words have upheld him that was falling, and you have strengthened the feeble knees. But now trouble is come upon you, and thou faintest; it touches thee, and you are troubled. Is not this your fear, your confidence, your hope, and the uprightness

of your ways? Remember, I pray thee, who ever perished being innocent? Or where will the righteous be cut off? It is as I have always seen. They that plow iniquity and sow wickedness, reap the same.

Job 4:1–8 (KRV)

Behold, happy is the man whom God has corrected: therefore, do not despise the chastening of the Almighty. For He makes a sore, and then He heals it: He will wound you, and His hands will make you whole.

Job 5:17–18 (KRV)

Eliphaz believes Job should be glad he is suffering because he thinks that punishment is all that is required for salvation. But what good is punishment if you do not know why you are being punished? Eliphaz doesn't appear to know that in order to be forgiven, we must first learn what our sin is and then ask to be forgiven for it. He must have also thought that forgiveness is automatic whenever you suffer, for he tells Job:

He shall deliver thee in six troubles. Yea, in seven there shall no evil touch thee. In famine He shall rescue you from death, and in war He shall protect you from the power of the sword. You shall be hidden from the lash of the tongue: neither shall you be afraid of destruction when it comes. At destruction and famine you shall laugh, neither shall you be afraid of the beasts of the earth. For you shall be in harmony with the stones of the field, and the beasts of the field shall be at peace with thee. And you shall know that your tabernacle shall be in peace; and you shall visit the place of your habitation, and shall not sin. Thou shall know also that your seed shall be great, and that your offspring will be as the grass of the earth. You shall come to your grave in a full age, like as a shock of corn comes in, in its season. Hear this, for we have searched it out, and so it is. Hear it, and know that the chastising from the Almighty, is for your own good.

Job 5:19–27 (KRV)

But Job answered Eliphaz and said, Oh that my grief were thoroughly weighed, and my calamity laid in the balances together to be weighed with my grief; For now it would be heavier than the sand of the sea. Therefore my words are swallowed up. For the arrows of the Almighty are within me, the poison whereof drinks up my spirit. The terrible things of God do set themselves in array against me.

Job 6:1–4 (KRV)

Isn't that just like some people today? They blame God or someone else for their problems when it's their own fault. Job continues:

> For now you are nothing; you see my casting down, and are afraid. Did I say, Bring yourself unto me? Or did I say, give me a reward of your substance? Or, Deliver me from the enemy's hand? Or, Redeem me from the hand of the mighty? Teach me, and I will hold my tongue. And cause me to understand wherein I have erred. Are not right words forceful? But what are you trying to prove with your arguing? Do you imagine to admonish me with words, and the speeches of one that is desperate, which are as wind? Yea, you overwhelm the fatherless, and dig a pit for your friend. Now therefore be content, look upon me; for it will be evident unto you if I lie. Agree with me, I pray you, let my words be not iniquity; yea, return my speech, for my righteousness is in it. Is there iniquity in my tongue? Cannot my taste discern perverse things?

Is there not an appointed time to man upon earth? Are not his days also like the days of a hireling? As a servant earnestly desires the shadow of rest, and as a hireling looks for the reward of his work: Like so, I am made to possess months of vainness, and wearisome nights are appointed to me. When I lie down, I say, shall I arise again? And should I say to the night, be gone? I am full of tossing to and fro, until the dawning of the day. My flesh is clothed with worms and clods of dust, my skin is broken, and has become loathsome. My days are swifter than a weaver's shuttle, and are spent without hope.

Job 6:21–7:6 (KRV)

Job gazes toward the heavens and asks:

O lord, how long will it be before you depart from me, and let me alone till I swallow down my spittle? If I have sinned; what shall I do unto Thee, O thou preserver of men? Why have you set me as a mark against Thee, so that I am a burden to myself? And why do You not pardon my transgression, and take away my iniquity? For now I shall sleep in the dust; and Thou shall seek me in the morning, but I shall not be found.

Job 7:19–21 (KRV)

Now, we'll hear from another one of Job's old friends.

Then Bildad the Shuhite answered Job, and said, How long will you speak these things, and how long shall the words of your mouth be like the strong wind? Does God pervert judgment or does the Almighty pervert justice? Your children must have sinned against Him, and He has cast them away for their transgression: If you would promptly seek out God and make thy supplication to the Almighty; If you were pure and upright; surely now He would rise up for you, and make your righteousness home prosperous. Though thy beginning was small, yet thy latter end should greatly increase.

Job 8:1–7 (KRV)

Behold, God will not cast away a perfect man, neither will He help the evil doers. Pray for forgiveness till He fills thy mouth with laughing, and your lips with rejoicing. Then they that hate thee shall be clothed with shame; and the dwelling place of the wicked shall come to naught.

Job 8:20–22 (KRV)

THE PATIENCE OF JOB

Before we continue the story, I would like to remind you that the wording of the Scripture has been revised and I encourage you to compare my interpretation (KRV) with the King James Version of the Holy Bible, which is used today.

Job may have patiently waited while his friends ridiculed him, but that would have been the extent of his patience. Now, I've always heard people speak of the patience of Job, but I find nothing whatsoever in Job's words that show him to be a patient man. It seems quite the contrary to me.

> Then Job answered Bildad the Shuhite, and said, I know it is so and a truth: but how should man be just with God? If he will contend with Him, he cannot answer Him one of a thousand.

He is wise in heart, and mighty in strength: who has hardened himself against God, and has prospered?

Job 9:1–4 (KRV)

For He breaks me with a tempest, and multiplies my wounds without cause. He will not allow me to take an easy breath, but fills me with bitterness. If I speak of strength, loe, He is strong: and if of judgment, who shall set me a time to plead? If I justify myself, my own mouth shall condemn me: if I say, I am perfect, it shall also prove me perverse. Though I were perfect, yet would I not know my soul: I would despise my life. This is one thing, therefore I'll say it; God destroys the perfect and the wicked. If this plague should suddenly slay me, He will laugh at the trial of this innocent man. God has given the earth into the hand of the wicked: He covers the faces of the judges thereof; if not, where, and who is He?

Now my days are swifter than a post: they flee away, they see no good. They are passed away as the swift ships: as the eagle that hastens to the prey. If I say, I will not forget my complaint, I will leave off my heaviness, and comfort myself. I am afraid of all my sorrows, I know that you will not hold me innocent. If I be wicked, why then do I labor in vain? If I wash myself with snow water, and make my hands never so clean; Yet you shall plunge me in the ditch, and my own clothes shall despise me. For God is not a man as I am, that I should answer Him, and we should come together in judgment. Neither is there any mediator between us, that might lay his hand upon us both. Let Him take his rod away from me, and let not His fear terrify me: Then I would speak, and not fear Him; but it is not so with me.

Job 9:17–35 (krv)

Do not overlook the significance of Job's complaining for the want of a mediator between him and God. According to the Apostle Paul in his first epistle to Timothy we now have an advocate: "For there is one God, and one mediator between God and men, the man Christ Jesus" (1 Timothy 2:5 kjv present-day).

Note: This next passage is what Job thinks he would say to God, if he had the chance. It's easy to boast that we're going to be bold, but reality is usually much different. – Job continues.

My soul is weary of my life, I will leave my complaint upon myself; I will speak in the bitterness of my soul. I will say unto God, do not condemn me; show me therefore why You struggle in opposition and dispute earnestly with me. Is it good unto Thee that You should oppress me, that You should despise the work of my hands, and shine Your light upon the counsel of the wicked? Do You have eyes of flesh? Or do You see as man sees? Are Your days as the days of man? Or, are Your years as man's days?

Job 10:1–5 (KRV)

Job poses a very good question here that is clearly answered in the second book of Peter. It is written: "But, beloved, be not ignorant of this one thing, that one day is with the Lord as a thousand years, and a thousand years as one day" (2 Peter 3:8, KJV present-day). When this passage was written, the count of a thousand was the largest number many could comprehend. If the same message were to be communicated today, it would most likely be written; be not ignorant of this one thing, that one day is with the Lord as a million years, and a million years as one day. Do not overlook the small word "as" for this tells us that the years of God are as countless as the sand in the sea. Now, Job is still telling us what he would say to God if they were to meet face-to-face.

Why do You inquire about my iniquity, and search after my sin? You know that I am not wicked; and there is none that can deliver me out of Your hand.

Job 10:6–7 (KRV)

If I sin, then You mark me, and You will not pardon me from my iniquity. If I be wicked, woe unto me; and if I be righteous, yet should I not lift up my head: I am full of confusion, therefore can You see my affliction? For it increases: You hunt me as a fierce lion: and then You show thyself marvelous upon me. You renew your witnesses against me, and increase Your indignation upon me; Changes and strife are against me.

Wherefore then have you brought me forth out of the womb? Oh that I had given up the ghost, and no eye had seen me! I should have been as though I had not been, I should have been carried from the womb to the grave. Are not my days few? Cease then, and let me alone that I may take a little comfort before I go to the place from where I shall not return, even to the land of darkness and the shadow of death; A land of darkness, as darkness itself, and of the shadow of death, without any order, and where the light is as darkness.

Job 10:14–22 (KRV)

Now it's Zophar's turn, and we find that he is just as angry with Job as his two friends are.

Then Zophar the Naamathite answered Job, and said, Should not the multitude of words be answered? And should a man full of talk be justified? Should your lies make men hold their peace? And when you mock us shall no man make you ashamed? For you have said, My doctrine is pure, and I am clean in thine eyes. But, oh that God would speak, and open His lips against thee, And that He would show you the secrets of wisdom, that your sins are double to that which is! Know therefore that God exacts of thee less than your iniquity deserves. Can you by searching find out God's will? Can you find out the perfection of the Almighty? It is as high as heaven, what can you do? Deeper than hell, what can you know? The measure of His perfection is longer than the earth, and broader than the sea.

Job 11:1–9 (KRV)

If iniquity should be in your hand, put it far away, and do not let wickedness dwell in your tabernacles. For then you shall lift up your face without spot, yea, you shall be steadfast, and shall not fear: because you shall forget your misery, and remember it as waters that pass away: And your age shall be clearer than the noonday after the rain; thou shall shine forth, thou shall be as the morning when all things are anew. Put iniquity from you, And you shall be secure because there is hope; yea, you will dig about yourself, and thou shall take thy rest in safety. Also thou shall lie down in peace, and none shall make thee afraid; yea, many will follow you. But remember this, that the eyes of the wicked shall fail, and they shall not escape, and their hope shall die and be as the giving up of the ghost.

Job 11:14–20 (KRV)

This conversation between Job and his three friends reminds me of how I became aware that there are people in this world who will judge you by your circumstance. It happened in the fall of 1959, the year I entered the ninth grade. That year, at the beginning of one of my classes, the teacher said, "We're not going to do like we did last year, this year we're going to buckle down and learn something." Then he said that we should get to know each other better by telling everyone a little bit about ourselves. After that, he started down the role asking, "What does your father do for a living?"

Now, for many of you, this will seem like an easy question, but for me it wasn't. Another student before me had a very tough time answering that question. The teacher humiliated him by continually asking him to speak up and by making sure everyone knew that he did not know who his real father was. Even after all this, the teacher didn't move on until he further established that state welfare helped support his family.

When he asked me that question, I answered, "He works on a canal."

"There aren't any canals in Oklahoma," he said. "Where does your father work on a canal?"

"In Idaho."

"Then your father doesn't live with you. Are your parents divorced?" I couldn't remember but I think I said, yeah or uh-huh, probably the latter. The teacher then asked, "Does your father send money?"

"Not much."

"Then what is your family's means of support?"

I was glad my last name started with an R, because I had time to figure out how to answer that question. Without hesitation, I answered very clearly with one word, "Welfare!" I had to answer that question three more times, because the teacher did the same thing each year. Now, I didn't have to take that course again, but it was a very easy credit, and I kept forgetting about that embarrassing question. Even back then, I knew they made fun of those on public assistance, because they talked behind that other kid's back! I had hoped to keep that little bit of information quiet.

It was moments like that which motivated me to improve my lot in life. And I quickly learned that if you want to get ahead, you must study hard and learn well. That habit of learning things very well is one of the things that led me to stay with the story of Job until I understood it. It is a very difficult story to comprehend; nevertheless, I have always found that the rewards of learning well enough to understand are always worth the effort. Now, I find that the Old Testament book of Job is actually an easy story to understand; it is just an exceptionally difficult story to learn. Okay, back to the Scriptures.

> And Job answered Zophar the Naamathite, and said, There is no doubt that you represent the people, and wisdom shall die with you. But I have understanding as well as you, I am not inferior to you: yea, who does not know such things as these? I am as one mocked of his

neighbor, who calls upon God, and He answers him: But the just upright man is laughed to scorn. He that is ready to slip into the grave, is as a wise man that is despised in the thoughts of him that is at ease.

Job 12:1–5 (KRV)

In other words: Lazy people will ridicule the hardworking, and the ungodly will scorn those who do good. Job continues:

The tabernacles of robbers prosper, and they that provoke God are secure, into whose hand God brings forth abundantly. But now, ask the beasts and they shall teach thee; and the fowls of the air, and they shall tell thee. Or speak to the earth, and it shall teach you; and the fishes of the sea shall declare unto thee. Who knows not in all these, that the hand of the Lord has brought this upon me? In His hand is the soul of every living thing, and the breath of all mankind. Does not the ear try words as the mouth tastes meat? With the ancient is wisdom; and in length of days understanding.

Job 12:6–12 (KRV)

Job admits that old men are wiser; now, he will speak of the wisdom of our Maker, for he says:

With God is wisdom and strength, He has wise counsel and understanding. Behold, He breaks down, and it cannot be built again: he shuts up a man, and there can be no opening. Behold, He can withhold the waters, and they dry up: also he sends them out, and they overturn the earth. With God is strength and wisdom: the deceived and the deceiver are His. He will lead counselors away spoiled, and make fools of the judges.

He loosens the bond of kings, and girds their loins with a girdle. He can lead princes away spoiled, and overthrow the mighty. He removes the speech of the trusty, and takes away the understanding of the aged. He pours contempt upon princes, and weakens the strength of the mighty. God discovers deep things in dark places, and brings the shadow of death to light. He increases the nations, and destroys them: He enlarges the nations, and contracts them again. He takes away the heart of the chief of the people of the earth, and causes them to wander in a wilderness where there is no way. They grope in the dark without light, and God makes them to stagger like a drunken man.

Loe, my eyes have seen all this, my ears have heard and understood it. What you know, the same I know also, I am not inferior unto you. Surely I would speak to the Almighty, and I desire to reason with Him. But you are forgers of lies, you are all physicians of no value. O that ye would altogether hold your peace, and that would be your wisdom.

Job 12:13–13:5 (KRV)

Does this ever hit home, because many a time I am talking when I should be listening. At the beginning, I said that God deceived Satan. Job just told us that the deceived and the deceiver are God's. This is just one of the passages that helped me understand the conversation between God and Satan at the beginning of the story. Job continues.

Hear now my reasoning, and hearken to the pleadings of my lips. Will you speak wickedly for God? And talk deceitfully for Him? Will you accept His person? Will you contend for Him? Is it good that He should search you out? Or as one man mocks another, do you likewise mock God? He will surely disapprove, if you do secretly praise a person. Shall not his Excellency make you afraid? And shall not His dread fall upon you? Your reminders of His deeds are like the ashes, your bodies are like bodies of clay.

Hold your peace, let me alone that I may speak, and let come on me what will. Wherefore I will take my flesh in my teeth, and put my life in my hand? Though He slay me, yet I will trust in Him: but, I will maintain my own ways before Him. He shall also be my salvation: for a hypocrite shall not come before Him. Hear diligently my speech, and my declaration with your ears. Behold now, I have ordered my cause, I know that I shall be justified. Who is he that will plead with me to God? For now if I hold my tongue, I shall give up the ghost.

Job 13:6–19 (KRV)

Job looks toward the heavens and begins speaking as if he is talking to God.

Do only two things for me: then I will not hide myself from Thee. Withdraw Your hand far from me: and let not Thy dreadful punishment make me afraid. Then call on me, and I will answer: or let me speak, and then You answer me. How many are my iniquities and sins? Make me to know my transgression and my sin. Why do you hide Your face from me, and hold me as Your enemy?

Job 13:20–24 (KRV)

Job has just asked God to make him know what he has done wrong. To ask a question like this is actually a good trait in one's personality. That is because so many of us will never consider that our problems might be our own fault. Now, Job is going to ask a question that many have asked, and I think he answers his own question. Some say that there will be a bodily resurrection. But I tend to agree with Job and believe that we will change into something else, maybe like the caterpillar worm that changes into a butterfly. Also, notice how Job's pride shows through in these next passages, as Job is sure that God will appreciate the work of his hands.

> If a man dies, shall he not live again? I will wait all the days of my appointed time, until my change comes. You shall call, and I will answer Thee: Thou will have a desire to see the work of thine hands. But, for now You number my steps, do You not watch over my sin? My transgression is sealed up in a bag, and Thou has sewn up my iniquity.

Job 14:14–17 (KRV)

Job is like a lot of us are today. He thinks that God will never reveal his faults because he can't see the truth, for his own pride has gotten in the way of his understanding.

JOB'S RIDICULE

We pick up the story where Job has just reasoned that if he has done something wrong, then there is no one who can tell him what it is. This is the second round of talks between Job and his three old friends, and we will begin with Eliphaz's second declaration to Job. Eliphaz slowly rises to his feet; he is very disgusted with Job.

> Then Eliphaz the Temanite said, Should a wise man utter vain knowledge, and fill his belly with the East wind? Should he reason with unprofitable talk? Or with speeches wherewith he can do no good? Yea, you cast off fear for God, and restrain prayer before Him. For your mouth utters your iniquity, and you have chosen the tongue of the crafty. Your own mouth condemns thee, and not I: yea, your own

lips testify against thee. Are you the first man that was born? Or, were you made before the hills? Have you heard the secret of God? And do you restrain wisdom for yourself only? What do you know Job, that we know not? What do you understand, which is not in us?

With us are both the gray headed and very aged men, much elder than your father. Are the consolations of God small with thee? Is there any secret thing with thee? Why do you let your heart carry thee away? And what does your eyes wink at, that you would turn your spirit against God, and let such words go out of your mouth?

Job 15:1–13 (KRV)

Note that Eliphaz is insinuating that Job is telling a pack of lies. It is common to see a person wink when they are about to say something that is likely to offend someone.

Eliphaz now turns to his friends and points an accusing finger at Job and says:

He shall not be rich, neither shall his substance continue, neither shall he prolong the perfection thereof upon the earth. He shall not depart out of darkness; the flame shall dry up his branches, and like the breath of his mouth he shall go away. Let not him that is deceived, trust in vanity: for self-esteem shall be his reward. It shall be accomplished before his time, and his branch shall not be green. He shall shake off his unripe grape from the vine, and shall cast off his flower as the olive does its fruit. For the congregation of hypocrites shall be desolate, and fire shall consume the tabernacles of those who practice bribery. They conceive mischief, and bring forth vain works, and their belly prepares deceit.

Job 15:29–35 (KRV)

Job's three friends have judged him to be wicked and vile because of his current situation. Way too many people will forget the good things about a man just as soon as it looks like he might have done something wrong. Now, back to the story where we find that Job is rising, even before Eliphaz is seated; he can't wait to speak.

Then Job answered, and said, I have heard many such things: you are all miserable comforters. Shall vain words have an end? Or, what emboldens you that you should answer? I could also speak as you do: if your soul were in my soul's place, I could heap up words against you, and shake my head at you. But I would strengthen you with my mouth, and the moving of my lips would assuage your grief. Though I speak, my grief is not assuaged: and if I should refrain from speaking, in what way am I eased? But now He has made me weary: God has made desolate all my company. And He has filled me with wrinkles, which is a witness against me: and my face bears witness to the leanness rising up in me. He tears me apart with his wrath, He who hates me: He grinds His teeth together in rage against me; my enemy sharpens His eyes upon me. They have gaped upon me with their mouth open; they have smitten me upon the cheek reproachfully, they have gathered themselves together against me. God has delivered me to the ungodly, and turned me over into the hands of the wicked. I was at ease, but He has broken me asunder, He has also taken me by my neck, and shaken me to pieces, and set me up for His mark.

Job 16:1–12 (KRV)

Do not overlook the fact that Job is blaming God for his problems. He is also very sure that none of this is his fault, for Job says:

But, not for any injustice in my hands: also my prayer is pure. O earth cover not yourself with my blood, and let my cry have no place in you. Also now, behold my witness is in Heaven, and my record is on High. My friends scorn me: but my eyes pour out tears unto God. O that one might plead for a man with God, as a man pleads for his neighbor. When a few years are come, then I shall go the way from whence I shall not return. My breath is corrupt, my days are extinct, the graves are ready for me. Are there not mockers with me? And does not my eye continue in their provocation?

Job 16:17–17:2 (KRV)

"And where now is my hope? As for my hope, who shall see it? They shall go down to the bars of the pit, when our rest together is in the dust" Job 17:15–16, (KRV). I believe Job is a little disgusted with his friends because he just told them, "If you are right, then you are going to go to hell with me." Now, we go to Bildad's second analysis of Job's situation.

Then Bildad the Shuhite answered Job, and said, How long will it be, O Job, till ye make an end of words? Mark, and afterwards we will speak. Why are we counted as beasts, and reputed vile in your sight? (Now Bildad turns to his two friends and says.) Job has torn himself in his anger: shall the earth be forsaken for him? And shall the rock be removed out of his place?

Job 18:1–4 (KRV)

His roots shall be dried up beneath and his branch shall be cut off above. Job's remembrance shall perish from the earth, and he shall have no name in the street. He shall be driven from light into darkness, and chased out of the world. He shall neither have son, nor nephew among his people, nor any remaining in his dwellings. They that come after him shall be astonished at his day, as they that went before were frightened. Surely such are the dwellings of the wicked, and this is the place of him that does not know God.

Then Job answered, and said, How long will you vex my soul, and break me in pieces with words? These ten times you have reproached me: you are not even ashamed that you make yourselves strange to me. And be it indeed that I have erred, my error remains with myself. If indeed you will magnify yourselves against me, and plead against me for my reproach: Know now that God has overthrown me, and has compassed me about with his Net. Behold, It is for this wrong that I cry out, but I am not heard: I cry aloud, but there is no judgment. He has fenced up my way that I cannot pass, and He has set darkness in all my paths. He has stripped me of my glory, and has taken the crown from my head. He has destroyed me on every side, and I am gone: and as for my hope, He has removed it like you would remove a tree.

He has also kindled His anger against me, and He counts me as one of His enemies. His troops come together, and raise up their way against me, and put an encampment around my tabernacle against me. He has put my brethren far from me, and those of my acquaintance are verily estranged from me. My kinsfolk have failed, and my familiar friends have forgotten me. They that dwell in my house, and my maids, count me for a stranger: I am an alien in their sight. I called my servant, and he gave me no answer; even though I appealed to him with my mouth. My breath is strange to my wife, she would not let me touch her. Even though I made an earnest request for the sake of more children of my body. Yea, the young children despised me; I arose, and they spoke against me. All my inward friends are hateful to me: and they whom I loved are turned against me. My bone cleaves to my skin and to my flesh, and I am escaped with the skin of my teeth. Have pity upon me, have pity upon me, O ye my friends; for the hand of God has touched me. Why do you persecute me as God, and are not satisfied with my flesh? Oh that my words were now written! Oh that they were printed in a book!

Job 18:16–19:23 (KRV)

Job doesn't know it, but the man that will see to it that his words are documented is listening. Job continues.

Oh that my words were graven with an iron pen and lead, inscribed in the rock forever! For I know that my redeemer is alive, and that He shall stand at the latter day, upon the earth: And even after I leave my skin, and worms destroy this body, yet in my flesh I shall see God: Whom I shall see for myself, and my eyes shall behold, and not another, though my reins, be consumed within me. But you should say, Why do we persecute him, seeing the root of the matter is found in me? You should be afraid of the sword: for wrath brings the punishments of the sword, and you know that there is a judgment.

Job 19:24–29 (KRV)

This is Zophar's last time to try to convince Job that he is a wicked man.

> Then Zophar the Naamathite answered Job, and said, Therefore, my thoughts cause me to answer, and for this I make haste. I have heard the check of my reproach, and the spirit of my understanding causes me to answer. Do you not know this of old, since man was placed upon earth, That the victory of the wicked is short, and the joy of the hypocrite but for a moment? (Zophar turns to his two friends and continues to incriminate Job.)
>
> Though his excellence mounts up to the heavens, and his head reaches into the clouds: Yet he shall perish forever like his own dung: They which have seen him shall say, Where is he? Job shall fly away as a dream, and shall not be found: yea, he shall be chased away as a vision of the night. Also, the eye which saw him, shall see him no more; neither shall he behold his place any more.
>
> Job 20:1–9 (KRV)

"He has swallowed down riches, and he shall vomit them up again" Job 20:15, (KRV). This is the portion of a wicked man from God, and the heritage appointed unto him by God.

But Job answered, saying, Hear diligently my speech, and let this be your consolations. Allow me to speak, and after that, when I have spoken, mock on. As for me, is my complaint to man? And if it were so, why shouldn't my spirit be troubled? Mark me, and be astonished, and lay your hand upon your mouth. Even when I remember that I will be justified, I am afraid, and trembling takes hold of my flesh. (Job is so upset with God that he begins reasoning that the wicked are treated better than he is. For Job asks.)

Why do the wicked live, and become old, yea, and are mighty in power? Their seed is established in their sight with them, and their offspring is before their eyes. Their houses are safe from fear, neither is the rod of God upon them. Their bull is fertile, and fails not; their cow calves, and does not cast off her calf. They send forth their little ones like a flock, and their children dance. They take the tambourine and harp, and rejoice at the sound of the organ. They spend their days in wealth, and in a moment go down to the grave. Therefore they say unto God, Depart from us; for we do not desire the knowledge of Your ways. What is the Almighty, that we should serve Him? and what profit should we have, if we pray unto

Him? Loe, their good is not in their hand: the counsel of the wicked is far from me.

Job 20:29–21:16 (KRV)

They shall lie down alike in the dust, and the worms shall cover them. Behold, I know your thoughts, and the devices, which you wrongfully imagine against me…How then can you comfort me in vain, seeing that there remains falsehood in your answers?

Job 21:26–27, 34 (KRV)

Job has just pointed out to his three friends that wicked people will prosper right along with the good and sometimes even better. He is also scolding them for accusing him of being a wicked person. No matter where you go in life, from time to time you will be confronted with people that will misjudge your character.

Job's Derision

Let's take a moment to review where we are in this story: Job's wife has cut him off, for Job said: "My breath is strange to my wife, she would not let me touch her, even though I made an earnest request for the sake of more children of my body" (Job19:17, KRV). All Job's closest friends have abandoned him, for he said: "All my inward friends are hateful to me: and they whom I loved are turned against me" (Job 19:19, KRV). His servants won't obey him. For Job said: "They that dwell in my house, and my maids, count me for a stranger: I am an alien in their sight. I called my servant, and he gave me no answer, even though I appealed to him with my mouth" (Job 19:15–16, KRV). Even Job's relatives will not have anything to do with him, for he said: "My kinsfolk have failed, and my familiar friends have forgotten me" (Job 19:14, KRV). And to top things off, the only friends that will speak to Job are still trying to convince him that his sufferings were brought on because of all the bad things that he has done.

As for Job, he had expected his old friends to comfort him with words such as, "Oh, you poor fellow, we have been praying for you. We brought you some herbs and oils to put on your sores, and all your friends are bringing pairs of oxen and camels and asses and sheep so you can rebuild your herds. Why, in no time at all, you'll be back on your feet and as good as new, and your beautiful wife tells us that she wants to have more children just as soon as possible." However, instead of bringing Job gifts or offering words of comfort, they ridicule him. And they haven't even given him as much as an old goat to help him replenish his once vast herds.

Job has every right to be angry with his three friends. Let us try to put ourselves in his shoes by considering something like this happens: Let's say the company you work for goes bankrupt and wipes out all the savings you had tied up in their stock, leaving you without a job or health insurance. Then all your children get killed in a freak accident. Then you get a curable form of cancer, but can't afford the treatment. Then to top things off, all your friends try to convince you that it's your fault because you don't go to church. In essence, this is how Job is being treated.

One of the things to be learned from this story is that some people will say things about you that are not exactly true. I picked up on this little detail because it has happened to me a few times. I have also learned that if you point this out to the person that is saying bad things about you, it can lead to a direct confrontation, and most often you will end up worse off than if you had just let it go. After this happened to me a few times, I decided that it was best to at least try to let it go and leave whatever should be done up to Jesus and His Father. That is after it dawned on me that what I should do is to follow the advice that Jesus gave us when He taught His disciples how to pray. It is this portion of the Lord's Prayer that finally sunk in me: "And forgive us our debts, as we forgive our debtors" (Matthew 6:12, KJV present-day). That means that if you do not forgive others for their transgresses, then God will not forgive you!

Now, let us get back to the story where two of Job's friends will try one more time to convince him that he is not the upright man that he thinks he is.

> Then Eliphaz the Temanite answered Job, and said, Can a man be profitable unto God? As he that is wise may be profitable unto himself? Is it any pleasure to the Almighty, that you are

righteous? Or is it an advantage to Him, that you make your ways perfect? Will He condemn you for fear of thee? Will He enter with you into judgment? Is not your wickedness great and your iniquities infinite? For you have taken a pledge from thy brother for naught, and stripped the naked of their clothing. You have not given water to the weary to drink, and you have withheld bread from the hungry.

Job 22:1–7 (KRV)

If you will return to the Almighty and repent for your evil deeds, thou shall be built up and you shall put away iniquity and keep it far from your tabernacles. Then you shall lay up gold as dust, and the gold of Ophir as the stones of the brooks. Yea the Almighty shall be your defense, and thou shall have plenty of silver. For then you shall have thy delight in the Almighty, and shall lift up your face unto God. Thou shall make your prayer unto Him, and He shall hear thee, and you shall pay your vows. You shall also decree a thing, and it shall be established unto thee: and the light shall shine upon your ways. When men are cast down, then you shall say, There is lifting up: and He shall save the humble person. He shall deliver the island of

the innocent: and it is delivered by the pureness
of your hands.

Job 22:23–30 (KRV)

In other words, Eliphaz says that God will only
deliver the pure and innocent from their affliction, and
that Job does not qualify.

> Then Job answered, and said, Even today my
> complaint is bitter: my stroke is heavier than
> my groaning. Oh that I knew where I might
> find Him! That I might come even to His seat!
> I would put my cause in order before Him, and
> fill my mouth with arguments. I would know
> the words, which He would answer me, and
> understand what He would say unto me. Will
> God plead against me with His great power?
> No, but He would put strength in me. There the
> righteous might dispute with Him; so should I
> be delivered forever from my judge. Behold, I
> go forward, but He is not there, and backward,
> but I cannot perceive Him.

Job 23:1–8 (KRV)

> My foot has held His steps, I have kept His
> way, and not declined. Neither have I gone back
> from the commandment of His lips; I have

esteemed the words of His mouth more than my necessary food. But He is in one mind, and who can turn Him? And what His soul desires, even that He will do. For He will perform the thing that is appointed for me: and many such things are with Him. Therefore I am troubled at His presence: when I consider, I am afraid of Him.

Job 23:11–15 (KRV)

Job is so sure that he hasn't done anything wrong that he begins reasoning that God gives to the wicked the same as he does to the righteous. For Job asks:

Why, seeing Times are not hidden from the Almighty, do they, that know Him not, see his days? Some remove the landmarks; they violently take away flocks, and feed thereof. They drive away the ass of the fatherless, they take the widow's ox for a pledge. The wicked turns away from the needy: the poor of the earth hide themselves together.

Job 24:1–4 (KRV)

Men from out of the city groan, and the soul of the wounded cries out: yet God does not accuse them of foolishness. They are of those that rebel against the light; they do not know the ways thereof, nor abide in the paths thereof. The murderer rises with the light and kills the poor and needy, and in the night he is as a thief. The eye of the adulterer also waits for the twilight, saying, No eye shall see me: and he disguises his face. In the dark they dig through the houses, which they had marked for themselves in the daytime: they know not the light.

Job 24:12–16 (KRV)

The womb shall forget the wicked man; the worm shall feed sweetly on him; he shall no more be remembered; and his wickedness shall be broken as a tree. He evilly treats the barren of child: and does no good to the widow. He also draws the mighty to him with his power: he rises up, and no man is sure of life. Though it be given the wicked to be in safety, whereon he rests; yet God's eyes are upon their ways. They are exalted for a little while, but are soon gone and brought low; they are taken out of the way as all others, and cut off as the tops of the ears of corn. And if it be not so now, who will make me a liar, and make my speech worth nothing?

Job 24:20–25 (KRV)

It takes a man with a lot of pride to be this sure of what he says! I know, because I can remember being sure of myself, even when I was wrong.

> Then Bildad the Shuhite answered, and said, Dominion and fear are with God, He makes peace in His high places. Is there anyone that can number His armies? And is there anyone upon whom His light does not arise? How then can a man be justified with God? Or how can he be clean that is born of a woman? Behold, to the Lord, even the moon does not shine, yea the stars are not pure in His sight. How much less then is a man, that is a worm: and the son of man which is a worm?
>
> Job 25:1–6 (KRV)

This is Job's final response to his three old friends, and I have not shortened it all that much. It is left mostly intact so that you will understand why I abridged the Old Testament Book of Job, so bear with me.

> But Job answered, and said, I have heard all your speeches, I pray thee: How have you helped him that is without power? How have you saved the arm that has no strength? How have you counseled him that has no wisdom? And how have you plentifully declared the

thing, to be just as you think it is? To whom have you uttered words or who do you think you're talking to? And whose spirit came out of you? Dead things are formed from under the waters, and the inhabitants thereof. Hell is naked before God, and destructive ways have no covering from His sight. He stretches out the North over the empty place, and hangs the earth upon nothing.

Job 26:1–7 (KRV)

He has taken away my judgment: and the Almighty, has vexed my soul, As God lives; As long as my breath is in me, and the spirit of God is in my nostrils; My lips shall not speak wickedness, nor my tongue utter deceit. God forbid that I should justify you: till I die, I will not remove my integrity from me. My righteousness I hold fast, and will not let it go: my heart shall not reproach me so long as I live. Let my enemy be as the wicked, and he that rises up against me be counted with the unrighteous. For what is the hope of the hypocrite, even though he has gained much, when God takes away his soul?

Job 27:2–8 (KRV)

Now, Job speaks of the value of wisdom and the meaning of understanding. He begins by asking:

> Where shall wisdom be found? And where is the place of understanding? Man does not know the price thereof; neither is it found in the land of the living. The depths of the earth said, It is not in me: and the sea said, It is not with me. Wisdom cannot be gotten for gold, neither shall silver be weighed for the price thereof. It cannot be valued with the gold rich land of Ophir, or with the precious gem of Onyx, or the Sapphire. The gold and the crystal cannot equal it: and it shall not be exchanged for jewels of fine gold. No mention shall be made of Coral, or of Pearls: for the price of wisdom is above Rubies. The Topaz of Ethiopia shall not equal it, neither shall it be valued with pure gold. (Then Job asks.)

Where then does wisdom come from? And where is the place of understanding? It is seen that wisdom is hid from the eyes of all living, and kept close from the fowls of the air. The devil and the spiritually corrupt say, with our ears, we have heard of the fame thereof. God understands the way of wisdom, and He knows the place of understanding. For He looks to the ends of the earth, and sees under the whole heaven: To make the pressure for the strong winds, and He measures the weight of the waters. He made a mandate for the rain, and a path for the lightning and a way for the thunder: Then God saw it, and did declare it, He prepared it, yea and He searched it out. And unto man He said, Behold, the fear of the Lord, that is wisdom, and to depart from evil, is understanding.

Job 28:12–28 (KRV)

Job is right in saying that those who fear God have wisdom. And I believe the first step toward wisdom is to learn the teachings of God and His Son Jesus well enough to understand.

JOB'S DECLARATION

Consider the content of the conversation between Job and his three friends for a moment and you will discover that mankind has not changed very much. Remember that Job began their meeting by complaining about his current situation, and even blamed God for it. Soon afterward, he justified himself by pointing out that God treats wicked men the same as He does the righteous. Then Job's three friends, who had intended to comfort him, decided to criticize him when they saw the extent of his infirmities. Remember how I said that we still have the same personality problems and that we treat each other in much the same manner. Is it not common to see someone size up a situation long before they have the complete story?

> Moreover Job continued his parable, and said,
> Oh that I were as I was in months past, as in

the days when God preserved me. When His candle shined upon my head, and when by His light I walked through darkness. Oh that I could be as I was in the days of my youth, when the secret of God was upon my tabernacle: When the Almighty was yet with me, and when my children were about me.

Job 29:1–5 (KRV)

Many of us are like Job and quick to elevate ourselves by bragging about the good things that we have done. After all, isn't that what we are doing when we tell others about our good deeds? We seem to forget that we are to keep our good works to ourselves. Jesus teaches us to look to our Father for rewards and not man. It is written:

Take heed that ye do not your alms before men, to be seen of them: otherwise ye have no reward of your Father which is in heaven. Therefore when thou doest thine alms, do not sound a trumpet before thee, as the hypocrites do in the synagogues and in the streets, that they may have glory of men. Verily I say unto you, They have their reward. But when thou doest alms, let not thy left hand know what thy right hand doeth: That thine alms may be in secret and thy Father which seeth in secret himself shall reward thee openly.

Matthew 6:1–4 (KJV present-day)

Back to the story, Job is still boasting.

When I went out through the gate to the city and when I prepared my seat in the street! The young men saw me, and hid themselves: and the aged arose, and stood up. The princes refrained from talking, and laid their hand on their mouth. The nobles held their peace, and their tongue cleaved to the roof of their mouth. When the ear heard me, then it blessed me; and when the eye saw me, it gave witness to me: Because I delivered the poor that cried, and the fatherless, and him that had none to help him. The blessing of him that was ready to perish came upon me: and I caused the widow's heart to sing for joy. I put on righteousness, and it clothed me: my judgment was as a robe and a crown. I was eyes to the blind, and I was feet to the lame. I was a father to the poor: and the cause which I knew not I searched out. And I broke the jaws of the wicked, and plucked the spoils of thievery out of his teeth. Then I said, I shall die in my nest, and I shall multiply my days as the sand.

My root was spread out by the waters, and the dew lay all night upon my branch. My glory was fresh in me, and my bow was renewed in my hand. Unto me men gave ear, and waited, and kept silence at my counsel. After my words they spake not again, and my speech dropped upon them. And they waited for me as one waits for the rain, and they opened their mouth wide as for the latter rain. If I laughed at them, they did not believe it, and the light of my countenance shown bright to them. I chose out their way, and sat chief, and dwelt as a king in the army, as one that comforts the mourners. But now they that are younger than I, have me in derision, whose fathers I would have disdained to set with the dogs of my flock.

Job 29:7–30:1 (KRV)

Few of us can resist the urge to brag, but we should be looking for ways to compliment others instead. Now, back to the story where we find Job is still complaining.

When I looked for good, then evil came unto me: and when I waited for light, there came darkness instead. My bowels boiled and rested not: the days of affliction came to me before their time. I went in mourning without the sun to comfort me: I stood up, and I cried in the Congregation. I am a brother to dragons, and a companion to owls. My skin is black upon me, and my bones are burned with heat. The music of my harp has also turned to mourning, and the sound of my organ into the voice of them that weep. I made a covenant with my eyes; why then should I think upon a maid? For what portion of God is there from above? And what is the inheritance from the Almighty on high? Is not destruction due the wicked? Is not a strange and fearful punishment due the workers of iniquity? Does He not see my ways, and count all my steps? If I have walked with vanity, or if my foot has hastily let me to deceit; Let me be weighed in an even balance, that God may know my integrity.

Job 30:26–31:6 (KRV)

Integrity is a very powerful word in the bible and is used quite often. For if you have integrity you will adhere to moral and ethical principles. You will be honest and have a good moral character. I think that it is prudent to mention that pride is not considered to be a part of someone that has integrity. Okay, back to the story where we find that Job is still bragging about how good a man he is.

If my step had turned out of the straight path, and my heart walked after my eyes, and if my hands were stained by evil deeds: Then let me sow, and let another eat! Yea let my offspring be rooted out. If my heart had been deceived by a woman, or if I had laid wait at my neighbor's door for his wife: Then let my wife grind upon another, and let others bow down upon her. For this is a heinous crime; yea, it is an iniquity to be punished by the judges. For it is a fire that would consume and destroy me, and it would root out all my increase.

If I despised the cause of my manservant or of my maidservant, when they disagreed with me; What then shall I do when God rises up against me? and when He visits me, what shall I answer Him? Did not He that made me in the womb make my servants? and did not someone fashion us in the womb?

Job 31:7–15 (krv)

If I had seen any perish for want of clothing, or any poor without shelter; If he that I helped had not blessed me, if he were not warmed with the fleece of my sheep; If I have lifted up my hand against the fatherless when I saw them begging at my gate: Then let my arm fall from my shoulder blade, and let it be broken from the bone. For destruction from God was a dreadful thing to me, and by reason of His highness I could not endure. If I have made gold my hope, or have said to the fine gold, You are the source of my confidence; If I had rejoiced because my wealth was great, and because my hand had gotten much; If I beheld the sun that it shined just for me, or if I said, it is by the moon's favor that I walk in brightness; And if my heart had been secretly enticed by riches, or my mouth had kissed my hand: This also would be an iniquity to be punished by the judge: for if I had done this I would have denied the God that is above. If I rejoiced at the destruction of him that hated me, or if it lift up my spirit when evil found him: Know that I would never have allowed my mouth to sin by wishing a curse on his soul.

Job 31:19–30 (KRV)

Oh that one would hear me! Behold, my desire is, that the Almighty would answer me, and that my adversary had written a book. Surely I would take it upon my shoulder, and bind it to me, and wear it as a crown. I would declare unto Him the number of my steps, I would go near unto Him as a prince. If the land had cried out, or the furrows thereof have likewise complained against me: If I have eaten the fruits thereof without paying for them, or had caused the owners thereof to lose their life: Then in my own land; Let the thistle grow in the place of wheat, and weeds in the place of barley. The words of Job are ended.

Job 31:35–40 (KRV)

Job and his three friends have made the same mistake that a lot of people make today. If they suffer or see someone else suffer, they blame God for it. Job may well have been the original self-righteous man, because even after all this tribulation, he still believes himself to be a perfect and upright man before God. His redeeming quality may be that he did consider that he might be doing something wrong, for he said, "Make me to know my transgression and my sin" (Job 13:23, KRV). And it is clear that Job's three friends still think his problems were brought on by his bad behavior. Neither of them considered that one's attitude could get you in as much trouble with the Lord as an outward act.

A YOUNG MAN'S WISDOM

Note: The Scripture from the 1611 edition of the King James Bible has been revised by the author. You are encouraged to compare passages marked (KRV) with the King James Version of the Holy Bible, which is used today.

The discussion between Job and his three friends has ended in the same manner that a lot of conversations like this do today. Everyone is upset and agitated and nothing whatsoever has been resolved. Job still believes that God is punishing him for no reason, and his three friends go on thinking that Job is suffering because he has done many wicked things.

The young man with them named Elihu was the only one that recognized Job's sin, and it is he that we will hear from next. Elihu will clearly show Job the flaw in his character and start him down the path to forgiveness. Many are like Job and believe that they are righteous, while others are like his three friends—ready to accuse and condemn at the drop of a hat. Some of us have both of these wonderful traits in our personalities and that makes us a most despicable person sometimes. It is a truly tough lesson that Job is about to learn. Stay with me, for the most important part of this story has yet to take place. Now, we return to the Old Testament story of Job where Elihu is about to show Job and his old friends the error of their ways.

> So these three men ceased to answer Job, because he was righteous in his own eyes. Then Elihu, the son of Barachel the Buzite of the kindred of Ram, became very angry, and his wrath was kindled against Job because he justified himself rather than God. And his wrath was also kindled against his three friends, because they had found no answer for Job's suffering, and yet they condemned him. Now, Elihu had waited till Job had spoken, because they were elder than he.

Job 32:1–4 (KRV)

Now, I picture Elihu rising and facing the three men, and they see that he is about to speak, so they get up. To remain seated while this young man speaks would show respect for him and his words. However, Job remains seated. Moreover:

> When Elihu saw that there was no right answer in the mouth of these three men, his anger was kindled. And Elihu, the son of Barachel the Buzite, answered them and said: I am young, and you are very old, wherefore I was afraid, and dared not show you my opinion. I say that, days should speak, and the multitude of years should teach wisdom. But there is a spirit in man: and the inspiration of the Almighty gives them understanding. Great men are not always wise: neither does the aged understand judgment. Therefore I say, hearken to me: I also will show you my opinion. Behold, I waited for your words: And I gave ear to your reasons, while you searched out what to say. Yea, I gave attention to your words, and behold, there was none of you that showed Job his error, or that answered his words: Unless you should say, We have found our wisdom: God thrusts him down, not man. Now, Job has not directed his words against me: neither will I answer him with more of your speeches. They were amazed, they answered no more: they left off speaking.
>
> Job 32:5–15 (KRV)

I made a comment earlier that I think the man that will document their words is listening. I said this because the story now takes on a first person point of view. This last passage also shows that Elihu was there all along. He was likely there to attend to the needs of Job's three old friends.

> When I had waited, (for they spake not, but stood still and answered no more;) I said, I will answer also on my behalf, I also will show you my opinion. For I am full of matter, the spirit within me compels me to speak. Behold, my belly is as fermenting wine, which has no vent, it is ready to burst like bottles of new wine. Therefore I will speak, that I may be refreshed: I will open my lips, and answer. Do not let me, I pray you, embrace any person: neither let me give flattering titles unto man. For I know that I am not to give flattering titles: in so doing my Maker would soon take me away. Elihu now directs his words to Job. Wherefore, Job, I pray thee, hear my speeches, and give ear to all my words. Behold, now I have opened my mouth, my tongue has spoken in my mouth. My words shall be of the uprightness of my heart: and my lips shall utter knowledge clearly. The Spirit of God has made me, and the breath of the

Almighty has given me life. If you can, answer
me, stand up and set your words in order before
me. Behold, I am according to thy wish in
God's stead: I am also formed out of the clay.

Job 32:16–33:6 (KRV)

In this last passage, *stead* means "instead of" or "in
the place of." It can also mean to be helpful to. I believe
Elihu is telling Job that he is speaking on God's behalf.
Ehihu continues.

Behold, my intense fear of God shall not make
you afraid, neither shall my hand be heavy upon
you. You have spoken as one sure of himself in
my hearing, and I have heard the voice of thy
words, saying, I am clean without transgression,
I am innocent; neither is there iniquity in me.
Behold, He finds occasions to punish me, He
counts me as His enemy, He puts my feet in
the stocks, He marks all my paths. Behold, in
this thou art not just: I will answer thee, that
God is greater than man. Why do you struggle
against Him? For He does not give account of
any of his matters. For God has spoken once,
yea twice, yet man did not perceive it.

Job 33:7–14 (KRV)

Did you ever wake up with a new understanding of something or knowing exactly what to do in a tough situation? Have you ever wondered why people will tell you to sleep on it? Pay close attention to what Elihu tells Job about how God communicates with us.

> In a dream, in a vision of the night, when deep sleep falls upon men, in the slumbering upon their bed; Then He opens the ears of men, and seals their instruction, That He may withdraw man from his evil ways, and hide pride from man. To keep his soul back from the pit, and his life from perishing by the sword.

Job 33:15–18 (KRV)

This was the turning point in Job's life because Elihu was finally able to show him that pride in oneself is a sin. Throughout the bible the words pride and proud are listed with words that describe the very worst aspects of human nature. Here is how our Lord Jesus looks on pride: "And he said, That which cometh out of the man, that defileth the man. For from within, out of the heart of men, proceed evil thoughts, adulteries, fornications, murders, thefts, covetousness, wickedness, deceit, lasciviousness, an evil eye, blasphemy, pride, foolishness: All these evil things come from within, and defile the man" (Mark 7:20—23 KJV present-day).

Elihu now turns to Job's friends and says:

If there were a messenger with him, an interpreter, one among a thousand, to show unto man his uprightness: Then God will be gracious unto him, and say, Deliver him from going down to the pit: For I have found a ransom for him. Job's flesh shall be fresher than a child's: he shall return to the days of his youth: He shall pray unto God, and He will be favorable unto him: and he shall see His face with joy: for He will render unto man according to his righteousness. He looks upon men, and if any say, I have sinned, and perverted that which was right, and it did not profit me; He will deliver his soul from going into the pit, and his life shall see the light. Loe, God works all these things oftentimes with man, To bring his soul back from the pit, to be enlightened with the light of the living.

Mark well, O Job, hearken unto me, hold your peace, and I will speak. If you have something to say, answer me: speak, for I desire to justify you. If not, give ear unto me: hold your peace, and I shall teach you wisdom. Furthermore Elihu answered, and said,

Hear my words, O yee wise men, and give ear unto me, ye that have knowledge. For the ear will try words, as the mouth tastes meat. Let us choose to use proper judgment: let us know among ourselves what is good. For Job had said, I am righteous: and God has taken away my judgment. And, Should I lie against my right ways? And, my wound is incurable, even though I am without transgression. What man is like Job, who drinks up scorning like water? Which goes in company with the workers of iniquity, and walks with wicked men. For he had said, It profits a man nothing, that he should delight himself with God. Therefore give heed to me, yee men of understanding: Far be it from God, that He should do wickedness, and from the Almighty, that He should commit iniquity. For He shall render unto him according to the work of a man, and cause every man to find rewards, according to his way. Yea, surely God will not do wickedly, neither will the Almighty pervert judgment.

Job 33:23–34:12 (KRV)

These last few passages are why I said that Job is one of those stories where the ending clears up what happens in the beginning. Satan would have left Job alone, but for the words of God. He focused Satan's attention on Job because, as we just learned, God will not do wickedness or commit iniquity. He needed Satan's help to teach Job a lesson in humility.

Elihu continues.

> He shall break countless numbers of mighty men into pieces, and set others in their place. Therefore God knows their works, and He will overturn them in the night, so that they are destroyed. God shall strike them as wicked men, in the open sight of others: Because they turned their back on Him, and would not consider any of His ways: So that they caused the poor to come and cry unto Him, and God does hear the cry of the afflicted. When He has given quietness, who then can make trouble? And when He hides His face, who then can behold Him? Whether it be done against a nation, or against a man only: Let the hypocrite reign not, lest the people be ensnared.
>
> Job 34:24–30 (KRV)

We should consider this last passage every time we vote for a leader, that is, because, a hypocrite will surely lead our nation astray. A good example of a hypocritical leader would be a man who purposefully avoided war himself, but then did not hesitate to send troops to fight in a war of his own making. Elihu continues.

Surely it is proper to say unto God, I have borne chastisement, I will not offend any more. That which I cannot see, teach it to me; If I have done iniquity, I will do no more. Should it be according to your mind? God will repay, whether you refuse or whether you choose to accept my words, and not I: therefore speak of what you know. Let men of understanding tell me, and let a wise man hearken unto me. Job has spoken without knowledge, and his words were without wisdom. My desire is that Job may be tried unto the end, because of his answers for wicked men. For he added rebellion unto his sin, he has clasped his hands together among us, and multiplied his words against God.

Job 34:31–37 (KRV)

I see Job's three friends as setting back down in a show of respect for Elihu, for I believe they are beginning to see the wisdom in this young man's words. There is also a stirring of dust in their midst as Elihu spreads one arm toward the three men and the other toward Job.

Elihu spake moreover to Job, and said, Do you think you were right when you said, My righteousness is more than God's? For you said, What advantage will it be unto me, and, What profit shall I have, if I be cleansed from my sin? I will answer you, and your companions with you. Look unto the heavens and see, and behold the clouds which are higher than thee. If you sin, what are you doing against God? Or if you multiply your transgressions, what are you doing for Him? If you are righteous, what are you giving to Him? Or what will He receive from your hand? Your wickedness may hurt a man as you are, and your righteousness might profit the son of man.

Job 35:1–8 (KRV)

Those that are oppressed will cry because of the multitude of oppressions: they cry out because of the arm of the mighty. But none has said, Where is God my maker, who gives us songs in the night? One who teaches us more than the beasts of the earth, and makes us wiser than the fowls of heaven. There the oppressed will cry out for an answer, (but none will be given) because of the *pride* of evil men. Surely God will not hear vanity, neither will the Almighty regard it. Although you say that you shall not see Him, know that judgment is before Him, therefore you must trust in Him. (Elihu now directs his words to Job's three friends.) But now because it is not so, God has visited Job in his anger, yet Job does not know the great extremity of God's compassion: Therefore Job has opened his mouth in vain: he has multiplied his words without knowledge.

Job 35:1–16 (KRV)

Remember that even Job did not know the great extremity of God's compassion. This simple lesson will help you understand the passages in the Book of John that were written about the disciple whom Jesus loved. Now, I picture Job getting up and beginning to pace about because Elihu's words are beginning to have an impact. He is very downcast and disheveled-looking.

Elihu also proceeded, and said, Allow me a little time, and I will show you that I have yet to speak on God's behalf. I will fetch my wisdom from afar, and will ascribe righteousness to my Maker. For truly my words shall not be false: he that is perfect in knowledge, is with me. Behold, God is mighty, and despises not any: he is mighty in strength and wisdom. He does not preserve the life of the wicked: but gives rightly to the poor. He does not withdraw his eyes from the righteous: but they are with kings on the throne, yea he will establish them forever, and they are exalted. And if they were to be bound in fetters, and to be held in cords of affliction: Then he will show them their work, and their exceedingly great transgressions. He will also open their ear to discipline, and command that they return from iniquity. If they obey and serve him, they shall spend their days in prosperity, and their years in pleasures. But if they obey not, they shall perish by the sword, and they shall die without knowledge.

Job 36:1–12 (KRV)

Hearken unto this, O Job: stand still, and consider the wondrous works of God. Do you know when God disposed them, and caused the light of his cloud to shine? Do you know the balancing of the clouds, and the wondrous works of Him which is perfect in knowledge? Do you know how your garments are made warm, when He quiets the earth by the south wind? Have you spread out the sky with Him, which is strong, and as a molten looking glass? Teach us what we shall say unto him; for we cannot put our speech in order, by reason of the darkness within us.

Job 37:14–19 (KRV)

Touching the Almighty, we cannot find Him out: He is excellent in power, and in judgment, and in plenty of justice: He will not afflict. Men do therefore fear Him: He does not respect any that are wise of heart.

Job 37:23–24 (KRV)

Elihu is making it very clear that man will never know all the ways of God. He is also making it very clear that God is all-powerful and that God's judgment is without question. And he is making it very clear that God will not punish man—that is, while we are still alive. But this does not mean that God will not let Satan have his way with us here on earth if we need to learn a very tough lesson.

GOD TEACHES JOB
AND HIS OLD FRIENDS

Let us remember that it was Elihu, who identified pride as being a very bad flaw in Job's personality, and that it was Elihu, who showed Job the error of his ways. Do not overlook the significance of the words of Elihu and the roll that he plays in the story of Job. Also, the wisdom that Job shows in listening to this young man is something that all of us need to consider. For when Job did not rebuke Elihu for his comments, God must have noticed that Job was beginning to learn his lesson, for the stirring of dust in their midst has turned into a whirlwind, and God Himself will now take over the discussion.

> Then the Lord answered Job out of the whirlwind, and said, Who is this that darkens

counsel by words without knowledge? Now you shall gird up your loins like a man; for I will demand of thee, and you will answer me. Where were you when I laid the foundations of the earth? declare, if you have understanding. Who has laid the measures thereof, if you know? or who has stretched the line upon it? Whereupon are the foundations of earth fastened? or who laid the corner stone thereof? When the morning stars sang together, and all the sons of God shouted for joy.

Job 38:1–7 (KRV)

Then God asks Job:

Have you entered into the springs of the sea? Or have you walked in the search of the depth? Have the gates of death been opened unto you? Or have you seen the doors of the shadow of death? Have you perceived the breadth of the earth? Declare if you know it all.

Job 38:16–18 (KRV)

Does the hawk fly by your wisdom, and stretch her wings toward the South? Does the eagle mount up at your command? And make her nest on high? She dwells and abides on the rock, upon the crag of the rock, and in the strong place. From there she seeks the prey, and her eyes can behold it from far off. Her young ones also suck up blood: and where the slain are, there is he.

Job 39:26–30 (KRV)

I picture that Job's three friends have risen to flee, but they cannot, for they are scared stiff, caught in the throes of panic. And, Job is beginning to look like a man that might have a little hope left. Nevertheless, his head is downcast and his hands are held out palms up, and he is facing the whirlwind.

Moreover the Lord answered Job, and said, Shall he that contends with the Almighty, instruct Him? He that blames God, let him answer it. Then Job answered the Lord, and said, Behold, I am vile; what shall I answer thee? I will lay my hand upon my mouth. I have spoken once, but I will not answer: yea twice, but I will proceed no further. Then the Lord answered Job out of the whirlwind, and said:

Gird up thy loins now like a man: I will demand of thee, and you shall declare your answer to me. Will you also disannul my judgment? will you condemn me, that you may be righteous? Have you an arm like God? or can you thunder with a voice like him? Deck yourself now with majesty, and excellency, and array yourself with glory, and beauty. Cast abroad the rage of your wrath: and behold every one that is proud, and abase him. Look on every one that is proud, and bring him low: and tread down the wicked in their place. Hide the proud and the wicked in the dust together, and bind their faces in secret. Then I will confess unto you, that your own right hand can save thee.

Job 40:1–9 (KRV)

Do not overlook the importance of these last four passages, because God has just informed Job that he can save himself by overcoming pride. Let us look at a passage from the New Testament that lists proud with words that describe some very bad aspects of human nature: "For men shall be lovers of their own selves, covetous, boasters, *proud*, blasphemers, disobedient to parents, unthankful, unholy, Without natural affection, trucebreakers, false accusers, incontinent, fierce, despises of those that are good, Traitors, heady, highminded, lovers of pleasures more than lovers of God;" (2 Timothy 3:2–4 KJV present day).

God is now going to tell us a little about His ways by comparing them to the traits of a mammoth.

The description very closely resembles that of an elephant, especially if you change the word *tail* to *trunk*. I changed the word because I suspect that the translators had never seen an elephant. They probably thought that if something on the end swings about, then it must be a tail. So try to visualize an elephant standing by a cedar tree with his trunk held straight up in the air. For if you could see the tapered trunk of an old cedar tree in my neighborhood, you would surely see the resemblance. Okay, back to the Scripture, God is speaking.

> Behold now the mammoth which I made with thee, he eats the grass as an ox. Loe now, his strength is in his loins, and his force is in the navel of his belly. He moves his trunk like a cedar: the unlimited strength and his weight are wrapped together. His bones are as strong pieces of brass: his bones are like bars of iron. He is the chief of the ways of God: Nevertheless, He that made him, can advance unto him with His sword. In other words: Despite the mammoth's great strength he is still subject to the will of God. Surely the mountains will bring him forth food: where all the beasts of the field play. He lies down under the shady trees, in the concealed shelter of the reed, and

marsh. The shady trees cover him with their shadow: the willows of the brook compass him about. Behold, he drinks up a river, and does not hurry: he trusts that he can draw up Jordan into his mouth. He takes it all in with his eyes: his nose pierces through snares.

Job 40:15–24 (krv)

In other words, he can see all that is going on and he can smell a trap. God gave us the parable of the mammoth to describe His ways, and now He is going to give us a parable of the creature that describes the ways of Satan. I thought God was talking about an alligator until I remembered that God said smoke goes out of his nostrils and a flame goes out of his mouth. God also tells us that there is none on earth like him and that Satan is made without fear. This is likely where the stories of a fire-breathing dragon came from. So try to visualize a fire-breathing dragon type of sea monster covered with fishlike scales thrashing through an angry ocean and in a hurry to…no place. God calls this creature Leviathan. God is speaking:

Can you draw out leviathan with a hook? or can you snag his tongue with a cord which you have let down? Can you put a hook into his nose? Or bore his jaw through with a thorn? Will he make many humble prayers unto you? will he speak soft words unto you? Will he make a covenant with you? will you take him for a servant for ever? Will you play with him as you would play with a bird? or will you bind him for your maidens? Shall your companions make a banquet of him? Shall they part him among the merchants? Can you fill his skin with barbed irons? Or his head with fish spears to slay him? Lay your hand upon him, remember the battell: do no more.

Job 41:1–8 (KRV)

Remember what I said about the word *battell*, which is pronounced as the word *battle*, and that it means a list of debts owed. God is telling us to hold Satan at bay and to remember that He is keeping track of Satan's debts, and for us to do no more than this. God continues:

Behold, the hope of him is in vain: One shall be overwhelmed even at the sight of him? There is not a person found, so fierce, that would dare stir him up. Who will prevent me from repaying him? Whatsoever is under the whole Heaven, is mine: Who then is able to stand against me? I will not conceal his parts, nor his power, nor his comely proportion.

Job 41:9–12 (KRV)

Loe, God is making it very clear that one day, He will hold the devil accountable for all his debts. God is also making it very clear that Satan will remain with us and that He will not conceal him from us. So we must learn how to recognize that handsome devil, for it stands to reason: if you do learn to recognize Satan, then he will not be able to influence you so easily. In this next passage a double bridle is a very strong bridle and we are asked who is there that can put it on Satan. God asks us:

> Who can discover the face of his garment? Or who can come to him with his double bridle? Or who can open the doors of his face? His teeth are terrible round about. His scales are his pride, shut up together as with a close seal. One is so near to another, that no air can come between them. They are joined one to another, they stick together, that they cannot be separated.
>
> Job 41:13–17 (KRV)

Now, as the scales, which he is so proud of, cannot be separated, even to let air in, too much pride may seal off our learning ability and make us hold to our preconceived notions, even when they are wrong! Here is another passage from the New Testament about the bad aspects of pride: "For all that is in the world, the lust of the flesh, and the lust of the eyes, and the *pride* of life, is not of the Father, but is of the world" (1John 2:16 ᴋᴊᴠ present-day) .Let us learn more about Leviathan. God is still speaking.

> By his sneezing a light does shine, and his eyes are like the eyelids of the morning. Out of his mouth go burning lamps, and sparks of fire leap out. Out of his nostrils goes out smoke, as out of a seething pot or caldron. His breath kindles the coals, and a flame goes out of his mouth. In his neck there remains strength, and sorrow is turned into joy before him.
>
> Job 41:18–22 (ᴋʀᴠ)

Do not overlook the significance of this last passage, "Sorrow is turned into joy before him." Satan enjoys your sorrow and he knows that his days are numbered, so he is going to have as much fun as he can in the meantime. So if you have wronged another and have not asked to be forgiven or if you refuse to forgive someone that has wronged you, then you will have sorrow; therefore, you will be making Satan happy. Apologize and forgive, then you will be happy, and Satan will be sorrowful. God continues.

The flakes of leviathan's flesh are joined together: they are firm in themselves, they cannot be moved. His heart is as firm as a stone, yea as hard as a piece of the nether millstone. When he raises himself up, the mighty are afraid: They know that he can break them apart, so they purify themselves.

Job 41:23–25 (KRV)

Upon earth there is none that is like him: who is made without fear. He beholds all high things: he is a king over all the children of pride.

Job 41:33–34 (KRV)

Let's take a close look at these last two passages: "Upon earth there is none that is like him: who is made without fear" (Job 41:33, KRV). Satan doesn't fear anything on earth, but we know that he fears God because he obeys His commandments. Remember that Satan couldn't do anything to Job until God gave him permission. Satan was first told that he could have his way with Job except, "Do not lay your hand upon him" (Job 1:12, KRV). Then Satan was told that he could have his way with Job, "but save his life" (Job 2:6, KRV). We know that Satan fears God because he did obey those commandments. We must learn to recognize

Satan, for anyone that is without fear is very dangerous and extremely foolish. This is certainly not the sort of being that you would want to follow. And let us look at the passage: "He beholds all high things: he is a king over all the children of pride" (Job 41:34KRV). This is a tough one to comprehend, because there are so many people that will tell you that you need to be proud of this or that. But the truth remains that if you are burdened with pride, Satan will be your king.

Now, we find that Job has remembered that God told him to gird up his loins like a man. So he has wrapped the sackcloth about his body in a manner that makes him appear noble. He is standing tall with his head up and arms outstretched and facing the whirlwind. His three friends are still trembling with fear. The young man named Elihu is beside Job. And remember that God told Job that he *shall* answer Him.

> Then Job answered the Lord, and said, I know that you can do every thing, and that no thought can be withheld from Thee. Who is he that can hide those who have counseled without knowledge? Therefore I have uttered that which I understood not, things too wonderful for me, which I knew not. Hear me, I beseech Thee, and I will speak: I will demand of Thee, and declare Thou unto me. I have heard of Thee

by the hearing of the ear: but now my eyes see
Thee. Wherefore I abhor myself, and repent in
dust and ashes.

Job 42:1–6 (KRV)

Job has just learned that God does not like his
children to be proud of themselves. Therefore, he told
God that he utterly detests himself, that he regards
himself with extreme repugnance, and that he will
repent by sitting in dust and ashes. Now, I picture all
five of them standing about the whirlwind, which is
now directly in front of Eliphaz. God is about to pass
judgment on Job and his three friends.

> And it was so, that after the Lord had spoken
> these words unto Job, the Lord said to Eliphaz
> the Temanite, My wrath is kindled against
> thee, & against thy two friends: for you have
> not spoken of me the thing that is right, as my
> servant Job has. Therefore take with you now
> seven young bulls, and seven rams, and go to
> my servant Job, and offer up a burnt offering
> for yourselves, and my servant Job shall pray for
> you, for him I will accept: lest I deal with you
> after your folly, in that you have not spoken of
> me the thing which is right, like my servant Job.

> So Eliphaz the Temanite, and Bildad the
> Shuhite, and Zophar the Naamathite went, and
> did according as the Lord commanded them:
> the Lord also accepted Job.

Job 42:7–9 (KRV)

Loe, God is making it very clear that they had to make burnt offering and bring gifts to Job, and that He will only accept prayers from Job for the forgiveness of their sins. Aren't we blessed that we now have Jesus as our Lord? Now, we can go directly to Jesus, and to God through Him.

Let's take a close look at what God told Job's old friends to do for the atonement of their sins. God told these men to go get seven young bulls and seven rams, which are all males (and in case you don't know it, a ram is a male sheep that has not been castrated), and give them to Job. They were also told to make burnt offerings as atonement for the words that they had spoken to Job. Then God told them that Job would pray for them, because He will only accept prayers from Job. And it is clear from this next passage that God put His hedge of protection back around Job after he prayed for his friends.

> And the Lord turned the captivity of Job, when
> he prayed for his friends: also the Lord gave

Job twice as much as he had before. Then all his brethren came there unto him, and all his sisters, and all they that had been of his acquaintance before, and they did eat bread with him in his house: and they expressed their pity for him, and comforted him over all the evil that the Lord had brought upon him: also, every man gave him a piece of money, and every one gave him an ear-ring of gold.

Job 42:10–11 (KRV)

Let us take a close look at the passage: "And the Lord turned the captivity of Job, when he prayed for his friends" (Job 42:10, KRV). Job was under the power of Satan right up until the moment he forgave his old friends for their evil words and prayed to God on their behalf. This is when God removed Job from the power of Satan and put him back under His wing.

I believe that Job and his wife are now looking much younger than their age, and I know this because Elihu said, "Job's flesh shall be fresher than a child's, he shall return to the days of his youth" (Job 33:25, KRV).

So the lord blessed the latter end of Job, more than his beginning: for he had fourteen thousand sheep, and six thousand camels, and a thousand yoke of oxen, and a thousand she asses.

He also had seven sons, and three daughters.
And he called the name of the first daughter,
Jemima, and the name of the second, Kezia, and
the name of the third, Keren-happuch. And in
all the land there were no women found to be
so fair as the daughters of Job: and their father
gave them inheritance among their brethren.

Job 42:12–15 (KRV)

It seems that Job was before his time in giving his
children, especially his daughters, an inheritance before
he died. The more modern belief is that you should
help your children materially while they are young. It is
only natural for your offspring to want to carry on the
same lifestyle that you provided for them. "After this,
Job lived an hundred and forty years, and saw his sons,
and his son's sons, even to four generations. So Job died
being old, and full of days" (Job 42:16–17, KRV).

This is the end of the Old Testament Book of Job,
and I hope you enjoyed the story of Job and have
learned a little more about the ways of God. To ensure
that you have learned all the lessons that are contained
herein, you will want to listen to and/or read the
story of Job again and again. Each time through it,
your knowledge of God's ways will increase, and the
passages will become easier to understand.

Loe, I know that one must not change the meaning of any of the passages in the Bible. And I want you to know that I was very careful to retain the original meaning of the Scripture in the abridgement and revision of this story as it is written in the original King James Version of the Old Testament Book of Job. And I hope that I have helped you learn and understand the story of Job, for if you learn this story well, it will give you one heck of an incentive to be the kind of person that God wants us to be. I say this because the punishment for Job's sin was brought to bear upon his first ten children, much more severely than upon himself. Remember that Job did not get into trouble because he lacked faith or because he was not trying to do the right thing. He got into trouble because he was full of pride, and he was without knowledge and understanding of the ways of God. Like Job, we too can get into trouble with our Lord if we are lacking in knowledge and understanding of the ways of our Father and His Son Jesus.

EPILOGUE

The Old Testament Book of Job teaches us about the many bad aspects of pride, but I think there is a time when pride might be appropriate. Here's an example: When I was in the navy and serving in Vietnam, my aircrew was given some time off for R&R (Rest and Recreation). A man named Chuck, another called Dalugee, and I rented a car and hired a driver to take us to a mountain resort in the Philippines. That evening, we asked our driver to take us to a nightclub where the locals went. We were having a good time until Dalugee got into an argument with the clientele and made some very derogatory remarks to and about the people that lived there.

When Chuck and I heard what was going on, we grabbed Dalugee and began a hasty departure. We made it to the car, but before we could get out of the parking lot, most of the patrons and employees of the club surrounded us. They were rocking the car, spitting on the windows, and calling us some very bad names. Our driver panicked and started screaming, "What do I do? What do I do?"

I replied in the calmest voice that I could muster, "Put it in reverse and ease back very slowly, but keep moving." Luckily, the huge crowd parted, and we were able to leave.

The next day, Chuck told me that we were going back to that place. I didn't think it was a very good idea, but he convinced me that we needed to go back and apologize to those people. Dalugee didn't want to, but we outranked him, so he went along with the idea. When we entered the establishment, guns immediately appeared on the bar and some of the tables. Dalugee turned to leave, but we took hold of him and marched him straight to the man that appeared to be in charge.

"This man has something that he wants to say to you!" Chuck told the man in charge.

Dalugee apologized, and then we did too. We turned around and headed for the door, but they caught us before we could get outside. I think we were all a little nervous until we understood that they wanted us to stay as guests of the house.

Later that evening, the owner of that nightclub told Chuck that he had seen a lot of servicemen get drunk and make an ass of themselves, but that we were the first to come back and apologize for it. We enjoyed their hospitality, and I think everyone there bought us a drink. That was a good lesson for me, because if it weren't for Chuck, I would not have returned to that place or even given a second thought about apologizing. So what does this story have to do with pride? Know that I am very proud to have served with the man that taught me what it means to be an American!

CLOSING COMMENTS

Loe, I have some comments to make that might raise a few eyebrows and upset some Bible scholars. Nevertheless, the spirit within me compels me to make these observations.

I have read and heard many erroneous comments about the Old Testament Book of Job. For instance, when a series of bad things happen to someone for no apparent reason, some will say, "He had a Job experience." Meaning, I suppose, that they think all the bad things happened to Job just to test or strengthen his faith, not because he did anything wrong. Job did sin, and his only sin was that of thinking way too highly of himself. God considered this pride to be a flaw in Job's personality and He wanted to correct it. This flaw was so deeply embedded that it took drastic measures to get Job to see it. Modern psychology teaches us that it takes a significant emotional event to change a person's behavior and that was the reason for God's words to Satan at the beginning of the story of Job. We know God needed Satan's help for Elihu said: "Therefore hearken unto me, ye men of understanding: far be it from God, that he should do wickedness; and from the Almighty, that he should commit iniquity" (Job 34:10 KJV present-day). God is not an evildoer, however Satan is and he enjoys your shortcomings. So if a friend points out a flaw, don't respond with: "I'm not that way" or "I don't do that". Always remember that God used Satan to help Him make Job see his faults! Now I say things like: "I'm better than I used to be", knowing that I still have a ways to go.

Learning to recognize pride in one's self is a very difficult task, but it can be done. Pride is that trait in our personality that will keep us from seeing our mistakes; therefore we are doomed to repeat them. Another bad aspect of Pride is that it will cause us to cling to our old beliefs even though they are not based on good judgment or sound doctrine. But worst of all and as the Book of Job teaches us, God will not forgive us for a particular fault until we know what it is and repent for it. After all, how can we change unless we know what we are doing wrong? And, we should always remember that: If we let our pride get too great,

Jesus just might point the devil in the direction of our doorstep, like as His Father did to Job.

Having pride in one's self may seem like a minor infraction of God's Law, but the truth remains; Job got into trouble with God because of his pride. Job was so proud of himself that he even mocked God by saying: "The tabernacles of robbers prosper, and they that provoke God are secure; into whose hand God bringeth abundantly" (Job 12:6 KJV present-day). Some people do have an abundant life without God by their side. They live as if they do not know that our time here on earth is just a fraction of our entire being. As for me, the evidence is overwhelming that we have a Creator. There's also plenty of evidence that there is an afterlife. My maternal Grandpa said it best when he wrote these words on Grandma's tombstone: "'Tis not the whole of life to live nor the all of death to die". I look on earth as being a proving ground where we are tested to determine whether we spend eternity in Heaven or hell. Oh yes, there is a hell, and the path leading there is bleak and rocky. That is because Satan enjoys your sorrow; and he will do whatever it takes to make you sorrowful, that is, if our Lord chooses to let him.

Another very important lesson, which is often overlooked in the conversation between Job and his three friends, is that you should never judge another. For a behavior, which you deem sinful, just might be an acceptable behavior before God. Jesus warns us that we have a tendency to put more restrictions on man than God does, for He said in Mark: "Howbeit in vain do they worship me, teaching for doctrines the commandments of men" (Mark 7:7 KJV present-day). Jesus teaches us that the testimony of two is true, so this passage is repeated in Matthew: "But in vain they do worship me, teaching for doctrines the commandments of men" (Matthew 15:9 KJV present-day).

The United States is becoming a nation that is full of proud people, and I'm not saying that as a compliment. If you think that we are not a nation of proud people, then consider the meaning of pride every time you watch a television commercial. The advertisers will play on your pride and vanity by telling you that if you buy their product, you will be sexy and cool and make all your friends envious. Some people will buy the more expensive automobile, or home, or clothes, even though they can't really afford them just to look good in the eyes of the world.

And then consider this: Many of the wealthy that already have more than most of us can comprehend will lie, cheat, and steal when their fortunes start to dwindle just so they can maintain their extravagant lifestyle. They are more inclined to serve their own vanity than they are to obey the law. Overcome pride and you will be a lot happier and much more satisfied with what you already have.

You should also note that God's law is just like man's law in a very important way. In that, ignorance of the law is never an excuse for breaking it. God must have known that many of His children would not have someone to teach His laws to them. So He put His laws into our mind, and wrote them in our hearts: "For this is the covenant that I will make with the house of Israel after those days, saith the Lord; I will put my laws into their mind, and write them in their hearts: and I will be to them a God, and they shall be to me a people" (Hebrews 8:10 KJV present-day). You must learn to listen to that small voice that we call a conscience, because that may well be God's way of letting us know when we are about to mess up. So don't argue with yourself when the body wants to do something that our mind tells us is wrong. Learn to pay attention to that small voice and it will save you from a lot of heartaches.

Someone will surely ask this question: If God's Laws are written in our mind then why do we need to learn the Bible? The people that ask this question are often the same ones that think they know what the bible says even though they have never truly studied the Bible. Since most of us will argue with ourselves to justify something we want to do, or have already done, we need to reinforce that small voice with knowledge of the written Word. And the only way to do that is to learn the Bible well enough to understand. It isn't easy, but like I said at the beginning: I have always found that the rewards of learning well enough to understand are always worth the effort.

Another thing: Why do so many preachers teach the Bible a passage at a time rather than a Book at a time? Many ministers of God's Word will jump around in the Scriptures so much that they miss the more important simple lessons. Some people have even skip-read the Old Testament Book of Job so much that they think the story describes God as a braggart, or that the story is about a battle between God and Satan over Job, or both. I find that it is easy to make a story come out to match your imaginations if you only skim through it. Then we have those that will rewrite the King James Bible just so they will have another book to sell. They don't even take the time to verify the accuracy of the Bible that they are rewriting. I wouldn't mind it so much if they would have at least made sure they understand the original version first. Some very important lessons have been changed and even lost in the later revisions of the original King James Version of the Holy Bible. This is just one of the reasons why any teacher of God's Word should study the oldest Bible that they are able to read. After all, common sense should tell you that the closer you get to the source of a story, the more accurate that version will be.

The Book of Job answers questions that many people ask when they suffer or see someone else suffer. Questions like, why is God doing these things or why is God letting this happen? Many inquiries about God that begin with why will be answered if you will only remember, that it was Satan who did all the evil things to Job, not God.

Now, if you are thinking that it is different after Jesus came, know this: Jesus only repealed about three of the laws of God. The other laws that Job lived under are still in effect. Jesus said: "Think not that I am come to destroy the law or the prophets: I am not come to destroy, but to fulfil" (Matthew 5:17 KJV present-day). Jesus teaches us that we no longer have to be circumcised, or make burnt offerings for the atonement of sins. And, we no longer need to have someone else pray for the forgiveness of our sins for we can go directly to Jesus and to God through Him.

Knowing these things will make many of the passages in the New Testament easier to understand.

Many Christians have oversimplified our relationship with the Lord! For if a prayer for forgiveness and the acceptance of Jesus as our savior are all that is required to get into heaven, then why is the Bible so full of lessons on behavior? They forget the passage in Matthew 11:29 where Jesus tells us: "Take my yoke upon you, and *learn* of me; for I am meek and lowly in heart: and ye shall find rest unto your souls" (Matthew 11:29, KJV present-day). I am afraid that prayer alone won't work for me, because I do not have a very good track record. I've already said too many things like: "Lord, I'll be good or I'll go to church from now on, if you will just get me through this rough spot". Now whenever I think about getting into heaven, the old saying "Talk is cheap, show me" comes to mind. You should not be too sure of your relationship with the Lord, for Job was sure of his place before God and look where it got him.

Loe, the Book of Job warns us that Satan watches over all high things and that he is a king over all the children of pride. So do not let your pride, which was the Sin of Job, get in the way of your understanding of any of the Scriptures in the Bible. And: Let not anyone else have to go through what an otherwise righteous Job had to go through to learn the error of his ways.

I thought I was finished with this book until I woke with this thought on my mind, so I got up and wrote it down. This is what I wrote: and unedited: — Through all these years God has gotten some awful bad press on account of two simple mistakes. You would have thought that the league of churches that recertified the 1769 edition of the King James Bible would have paid more attention to getting the job done right! — I was also reminded of something Elihu said: "In a dream, in a vision of the night, when deep sleep falleth upon men, in slumberings upon the bed; Then he openeth the ears of men, and sealeth their instruction, That he may withdraw man from his purpose, and hide pride from man. He keepeth back his soul from the pit, and his life from perishing by the sword" (Job 33:15–18 KJV, present-day). Thank you for reading and/or listening to this book.